OSPREY AIRCRAFT OF THE ACES • 20

German Night Fighter Aces of World War 2

SERIES EDITOR: TONY HOLMES

OSPREY AIRCRAFT OF THE ACES • 20

German Night Fighter Aces of World War 2

Jerry Scutts

Front cover
Heinz-Wolfgang Schnaufer,
top-scoring pilot of the *Nachtjagd*,
manoeuvers his Bf 110G-4 into his
favoured attacking position prior to
shooting down yet another
Lancaster on the way to achieving
his final tally of 121 kills. Schnaufer
preferred to attack the Avro bomber
from directly astern, where 'its
exhaust pattern could be seen from
2500 ft away'
(cover artwork by Iain Wyllie)

First published in Great Britain in 1998 by Osprey Publishing,
Elms Court, Chapel Way, Botley, Oxford, OX2 9LP

Reprinted Autumn 1998

ISBN 1 85532696 5

Edited by Tony Holmes
Page design by TT Designs, T & S Truscott
Cover Artwork by Iain Wyllie
Aircraft Profiles by John Weal
Figure Artwork by Mike Chappell
Scale Drawings by Mark Styling

Printed in China

EDITOR'S NOTE
To make this best-selling series as authoritative as possible, the editor would be
extremely interested in hearing from any individual who may have relevant photographs, documentation or first-hand experiences relating to the elite pilots,
and their aircraft, of the various theatres of war. Any material used will be fully
credited to its original source. Please write to Tony Holmes at 10 Prospect
Road, Sevenoaks, Kent, TN13 3UA, Great Britain.

CONTENTS

As arguably the most consistently effective arm of the wartime Luftwaffe, the *Nachtjagd* (night fighter force) took a steady toll of Allied aircraft – the vast majority of them RAF bombers – throughout most of World War 2. Fighting a tough enemy, as well as a lower priority in aircraft and personnel procurement than it merited, the force never shrank from its task. This initially remained frustrating for the crews because the very existence of a defensive night fighter arm was anathema to the creed of the Third Reich, whose leaders demanded almost totally offensive operations from the Luftwaffe. Ex-*Zerstörer* crews who provided the nucleus of the *Nachtjagd* even had the feeling that such a posting was tantamount to punishment. At a time when the Luftwaffe was confidently poised to attack England, and presumably cover itself with more glory in combat with the RAF, here were fully trained men being diverted from exciting daytime combat with a worthy adversary. But as the disastrous, and protracted, *Kanalkampf* (Battle of Britain) unfolded, *Zerstörer* crews soon realised that a transfer to the Nachtjagd probably saved their lives.

RAF bomber losses to night fighters increased, but for the Germans, the task of destroying the raiders was far from as easy as it might have appeared to the hapless Blenheim, Whitley, Wellington and Hampden crews who were on the receiving end. The first successful night fighter crews were ably assisted by their colleagues on the ground who manned the searchlights and flak batteries.

Bomber Command's expansion with better aircraft was met with German night fighters fitted with airborne interception radar which dramatically increased the chances of 'sure kills'. But try as they might, the defenders were rarely able to raise the loss ratio to more than ten per cent of the attacking force. This meant that far too many bombers always got through to devastate German cities night after night, week after week, under the British war cabinet's area bombing policy. This offensive, coupled with the attentions of American bombers by day, slowly, but surely, sapped the ability of German industry to sustain the war effort.

As with other branches of the Luftwaffe, the *Nachtjagd* created its *Experten*, a select band of pilots who rose above the rank and file, due in no small part to the efforts of their Bordfunkeren (radar/radio operators), who guided them into position to make sure of a kill. It was also the lot of these crews – such was the predicament the Luftwaffe found itself in – to fight on until attrition, or exhaustion, finally wore them down.

This volume is in no way intended to be a detailed history of the *Nachtjagd*, but instead concentrates on some of the operational techniques used and the experiences of a number of its leading crews.

WITH LIGHTS AND GUNS

Sharkmouths adorned numerous wartime aircraft, few as strikingly as the gaping 'Haifisch' jaws on the Bf 110s of II./ZG 76, the source of many aircraft and crews for NJG 1. In this view a Bf 110C is ticking over under a camouflage net. The sharkmouth marking was retained for some time on individual ZG 76 aircraft transferred to the night fighter arm – in individual cases with the white teeth oversprayed in black, the latter shade being the standard colour for night fighters in the early war years. Sharkmouthed Bf 110s formerly of II./ZG 76 seemed to provide the *Nachtjagd* with the bulk of its strength, although this was probably because they were felt to be more photogenic than plain black aircraft when it came to generating positive propaganda about the Luftwaffe's new fighting force! (*Hans-Joachim Jabs*)

Low-key Germany experiments into the visual night interception of enemy bombers had been conducted during the latter stages of World War 1. These were resurrected after the formation of the Luftwaffe in 1935, and a series of tests using single-engined fighters – notably the Arado Ar 68, Heinkel He 112 and Messerschmitt Bf 109 – showed encouraging, but inconclusive, results. If co-ordinated well with searchlights, and enjoying reliable radio communications, pilots were able, with some ease, to catch up with slow bombers, close with them and more often than not show that in a real combat situation they could have shot them down. Flak units, as part of the Luftwaffe, would, it was felt, play a significant co-operative part in destroying night raiders. Not that many Luftwaffe officers from Reichsmarschal Hermann Göring down believed this would really be necessary.

This thinking overlooked an international pre-war preoccupation with the bomber – air forces were built around offensive striking forces, the Royal Air Force and the Luftwaffe, being no exception. While the German air arm opted to build a force of short-range medium bombers, Britain's bombers were designed with a greater emphasis on range and the capability to reach targets in Germany. They were also as modern – particularly in their power-driven defensive gun turrets – as similar types anywhere, and on 3 September 1939, Bomber Command had 23 frontline squadrons with about 280 aircraft.

The RAF began attacking selected targets in daylight from the outbreak of hostilities, the Germans reacting with an integrated defence network of radar detection, fighters and guns, which resulted in some successful interceptions of bombers, usually in conditions of poor visibility during daylight hours rather than at night. Losses led to a British policy of night rather than daylight bombing, although 'cloud cover' operations would continue for some time.

German fighter defence in the early months of the war was vested in the Bf 109, and outstanding day fighter though it was, it was hardly the most reliable aircraft for night interception sorties. Operating in conjunction with searchlights, the flat perspex panels of the cockpit canopy would reflect glare so effectively that the unfortunate occu-

pant could hardly see out. Pilots were obliged to remove the side-opening canopy section in order to have any visibility at all on some sorties.

With all the emphasis placed on attack, the Luftwaffe had reserved few aircraft to undertake a night fighter role on the outbreak of war. Extensive pre-war reorganisation had seen a number of fighter units with some practical experience of nocturnal interception reduced to a single *Gruppe*, namely IV.(*Nacht*)/JG 2 equipped with the Bf 109D. A *Staffel* of this unit moved into Aalborg airfield on completion of the invasion of Denmark in April 1940 in order to share the facilities with the Bf 110Cs of I./ZG 76 and Wolfgang Falck's I./ZG 1. The airfield was soon subjected to attacks by RAF bombers, and these units flew interceptions during the early morning and late evening hours when natural light prevailed.

Falck found that fighters with positive GCI instructions resulting from plots on ground radar could be vectored accurately onto enemy bombers. The few RAF aircraft caught and shot down by what was basically an airfield defence force were enough to convince Falck and other pilots such as Werner Streib, Walter Ehle and Martin Lutz, that the Bf 110 could become an effective night fighter. Falck had scant little time to prove his theories as ZG 1 was transferred to Gutersloh in May, but he took the time to prepare a comprehensive report. This was well received and unwittingly marked out Falck as a leading authority on night fighting.

Wolfgang Falck, the first commanding officer of NJG 1. Surprised at the high command's perception of his knowledge of night fighting following a simple report on I./ZG 1's exploits in Scandinavia in April/May 1940, Falck nevertheless took up his new post with both drive and enthusiasm, helping him shape the *Nachtjagd* into a deadly force (*Toliver*)

SMALL BEGINNINGS

Despite a considerable effort on the part of Bomber Command crews, early flights into Germany were largely of the 'nuisance' variety. They served as a boost to British morale, proof that the nation was striking back at the enemy in virtually the only way possible on a regular basis at that time. The Germans themselves, previously amazed at the British showering the country not with bombs but propaganda leaflets, were nevertheless aware that enemy aircraft were able to penetrate their airspace with impunity. But a small-scale raid by 37 aircraft on Monchengladbach on 11/12 1940 May had seen high explosives aimed at a German town for the first time.

Then on 15/16 May the RAF carried out the first strategic bomber operation against German industry. Sixteen targets in the Ruhr were targeted by 99 bombers, the number despatched exceeding 100 (also for the first time) as 12 aircraft were also briefed to attack enemy communications points in Belgium. Little damage was done, and no bombers were brought down by hostile action.

In those days there was little attempt to send Blenheims, Hampdens, Whitleys and Wellingtons over Germany in formations, waves or streams. Crews tended to work individually, little knowing that they were making themselves ideal, albeit quite random, targets for night fighters. From their viewpoint the threat was perceived as minimal, and it was widely believed that losses were almost entirely due to flak.

Early German night interception doctrine, such as it was, followed more or less the broad parameters established in World War 1, and enforced during the pre-war experiments. As searchlights had then been a 'traditional' part of the night interception process, there appeared little need to change it in 1940. Consequently, when the first night fighter unit was formed, a searchlight regiment was concurrently allocated to it, along with a *Geschwader* headquarters. Ground radars were being produced at a steadily increasing rate and being installed to cover all the approaches to Reich territory likely to be taken by enemy bombers.

Bavarian-born Oberst Josef Kammhuber was chosen to oversee the establishment of *Nachtjagdgeschwader* 1, OKL (*Oberkommando der Luftwaffe*) having formerly created the post of 'Air Officer for Night Fighters' on the Luftwaffe General Staff. This carried far more responsibility than the title might imply. It meant that the officer was responsible for materiel procurement, pilot training, ground control, personnel and so forth. Kammhuber, who had been a Ju 88 pilot and *Kommodore* of KG 51, shouldered this additional responsibility with few qualms. He was a brilliant organiser and a good staff officer, used to reporting directly to (and dealing with) Reichsmarschall Göring.

Kammhuber's initial night fighter crews and aircraft would be drawn from the *Zerstörergeschwader*, which meant that the Bf 110 almost coincidentally became the primary night fighter type. There really was little else with anywhere near the performance required, although in mid-1940 this did not need to be exactly outstanding to catch the intended prey. For the record, the principal RAF bombers of that period could achieve the following maximum speeds in loaded condition: 235 mph for the Wellington, 192 mph for the Whitley and 254 mph for the Hampden. Of these the Wellington, considered Britain's most capable bomber, carried the largest bomb load and had the best service ceiling at 18,000 ft.

By contrast, the Bf 110C was capable of a maximum speed of 349 mph and a ceiling of 32,811 ft – so it can be seen that the interception of enemy bombers was not overly difficult if the searchlight batteries could follow them, and the night fighter was rapidly guided to the right sector to bring it within visual range. Not that the Bf 110 was the only choice of aircraft for the night fighter arm. Once the broad parameters had been established, numerous tests were conducted, not only of equipment with which to ease the crews' task, but other aircraft that could be adapted to the nocturnal interception role. Variants of the standard Dornier bombers were selected for conversion for a night role, these initially being the Do 17Z and Do 215B.

Bomber types, while large enough to house a four- to five-man crew, bulky radio equipment and ample guns and ammunition in new 'solid' nose sections, were considered to be too slow to be effective night interceptors, as they also lacked manoeuvrability and were excessively heavy. Nevertheless, the earlier Dorniers became useful workhorses and testbeds for equipment, as well as filling an operational need on a limited basis.

Much better all round was the Ju 88C-2, which was reckoned to be generally good for night interception because of its five-hour endurance – the fact that it could be crewed by up to four men, one of whom could act as a specialised radio operator, was another major consideration. In this latter respect it was superior to the Bf 110, which although it could, and did, accommodate a third man, became very crowded as a result. Also, an extra pair of eyes very usefully multiplied visual observation, which the Germans put great faith in for night fighting throughout the war.

Some crews did, however, resent changing over from the Bf 110 to the Ju 88, as the latter was a heavier aircraft lacking the performance of the lighter Messerschmitt 'twin' – in the main it came to be regarded as the second standard night fighter type after the Bf 110. Many embryo night fighter crews already knew the *Zerstörer* intimately, had flown it on daylight operations, and were thoroughly versed in its characteristics – most of which they found favourable.

The Bf 110 was endowed with a good rate of climb, being fast enough to catch any of the British night raiders and bring them down with its formidable cannon and machine gun armament, grouped in the nose to give an excellent concentration of fire. All German night fighters were well armed with a combination of cannon and machine guns, and while there were few complaints about firepower, individual crews showed preferences in the number of guns they wanted, and the type of ammunition to use.

Opinions understandably varied, particularly as to the effectiveness of heavy versus lighter cannon and the minimum number of such guns required. An important factor was to avoid the pilot's night vision being ruined by extensive flash when the guns were fired.

The early individualistic approach to night fighting tended to endure throughout the war despite new weapons installations. These inevitably led to the adoption of differing gunnery techniques, a fact that would later have a detrimental effect on the development of the Heinkel He 219. Having quizzed crews on their armament preferences in the 'ideal' night fighter, manufacturers had to cope with numerous conflicting requirements that could not always be easily reconciled.

The Bf 110s flown by NJG 1 were virtually standard aircraft, simply re-marked and repainted black for their nocturnal sorties. Black paint was also applied to *Nachtjagd* Ju 88s and Do 17s for in 1940 a dark colour was internationally believed to offer the best camouflage for aircraft operating at night, although this was later found not to be as effective as shades that were almost the complete opposite – light greys and white. But until 1943, the *Nachtjagd* would fly generally black-painted aircraft.

NEW EMBLEM

To engender *esprit de corps*, the *Nachtjagd* required an appropriate badge of identity. Wolfgang Falck was instrumental in getting this organised;

'While I was *Gruppenkommandeur* of I./ZG 1 in the spring of 1940, my idea was to have an emblem which should be a symbol – something to give crews the feeling that they were members of a special unit. There was a design competition, and I got several proposals. In my opinion the best one was submitted by Oberleutnant Victor Mölders, brother of the famous Werner. It showed the silver falcon taken from my family coat of arms with sky background that was then blue. Since we flew only against the RAF, Mölders included a red lightning flash pointing at London, the badge showing the section of the globe over which we were flying. A short time after this, I got the order to organise NJG 1, and I took the new badge with me. For the night mission, we changed the sky blue background to black. That was the origin of the *Nachtjagd-Abzeichen*, which was used by all the night fighter units, including the *Flakschweinwerfer Regimenter*, the *Luftnachrichten-Regimenter* and all staff echelons, with a few changes to demonstrate their special task.'

The 'England blitz' badge was very widely applied to *Nachtjagd* aircraft, and even when fresh *Staffeln* formed, or new *Geschwaderen* and individual emblems were applied, the badge remained predominant. In this small way the force indeed stood a little apart from other Luftwaffe formations, as was Falck's original intention for his unit, albeit one that had changed from day to night operations. The badge was also painted on equipment and vehicles as well as aircraft, including training gliders.

Victor Mölders, brother of then leading fighter ace Werner, designed the 'Englandblitz' badge seen here on a Bf 110 at Deelen. Universally applied to *Nachtjagd* aircraft and equipment, the badge was initially intended for ZG 1's *Zerstörers*, but was easily adapted for use by the night fighter arm through the simple expedient of changing some of the colours. The diving eagle was inspired by Wolf Falck's family coat of arms (*Falck*)

The importance of searchlights in successful night fighting was reflected in the addition of three white beams to the *Nachtjagd* badge by the searchlight units. This adapted emblem was painted on aircraft, notably Dorniers, flown by the *Nachtjagd* general staff, as frontline night fighters appear to have carried a badge without searchlights.

With the Luftwaffe high command recognising the urgent need for a night fighter force, Wolfgang Falck and others set about honing the necessary technique needed to bring down enemy bombers – not that destruction was initially the only option. It was thought, somewhat optimistically, that it might be possible to drive the bombers away from their intended objective. This quickly proved to be unrealistic.

Falck's earlier experiments into the feasibility of night interception, and his subsequent report, proved useful – and positive to the young Hauptmann's career, as he was appointed *Kommodore* of NJG 1 on 26 June. It was the first time that anyone of that rank had been given such responsibility. Falck, universally known by the shortform 'Wolf', did not minimise the difficulties facing *Nachtjagd* crews. Asked to make a parallel as to how the early pre-airborne radar interception sorties were conducted – one that might be readily understood by the layman – he said, 'Switch off all the lights in the room and try to catch a fly with your hands'.

This rare shot shows Bf 110s of 5.*Staffel* NJG 1 in Norway. The nearest machine seems to have retained light-coloured rudders, doubtlessly inherited from its 1940 *Zerstörer* day fighter camouflage scheme (*Knut Maesel*)

And that report he wrote had its repercussions. His rueful comment was, 'Of course when the first raids on Germany occurred it was my fault, you see!' Falck had previously discussed the outline requirements of a night fighter force with Göring, State Secretary Erhard Milch, Ernst Udet (the chief of Luftwaffe Supply) and Albert Kesselring. The latter had apparently demanded such a force be established forthwith when he had witnessed RAF bombers passing over his headquarters while he was C-in-C of *Luftflotte 2* for the assault on England.

To enable the various elements of a night defence system to be properly organised, a Night Fighter Division was set up on 17 July 1940 with Oberst Kammhuber in command. On the 23rd a Divisional HQ had been established at Brussels, and a command post was operational at Zeist, near Utrecht, by 1 August.

A ZG 76 Bf 110C clearly showing the typical application of the II.*Gruppe* sharkmouth, camouflage demarcation lines and code letters denoting, in this case, 5.*Staffel*. Under the aircraft's cockpit can just be seen the first of eight flags which represented the nations that ZG 76's crews had fought against by mid-1940 – this complex marking adorned all *Staffel* aircraft. Bf 110s in the same basic markings were transferred to the *Nachtjagd* in the autumn of 1940 (*Jarrett*)

The first *Gruppe* of NJG 1 was officially formed on 22 June with Falck in command. The basis was 2. and 3./ZG 1 and IV./ZG 26, and over the remaining months of 1940, the *Nachtjagd* grew rapidly. A second *Gruppe* of NJG 1 had originally been formed from IV.(N)/JG 2 on the same day in June, but in July this unit became III./NJG 1.

A second formation of II.*Gruppe* was created from (Z)./KG 30 in July, and when this became I./NJG 2 in September, a third formation of NJG 1 was concurrently organised that from elements of I./ZG 26. A typical example of the Luftwaffe system whereby experienced elements were transferred to create new units, this process was continued throughout the existence of the *Nachtjagd*. As all the *Zerstörer* formations, with the exception of KG 30, flew the Bf 110, this became NJG 1's standard aircraft, although its overall *Geschwader* inventory, in common with most of the *Nachtjagd*, would eventually include examples of all the leading night fighter types.

The *Zerstörer Staffel* of KG 30, in common with the rest of the *Kampfgeschwader*, was equipped with the Ju 88. When it moved to Dusseldorf to become 4./NJG 1 it set something of a precedent in that the *Staffel* thereafter operated a mix of Ju 88s, Bf 110s and Dorniers.

When NJG 2 was created in September 1940 its primary type was the Ju 88C, but the inventory also included the single Do 17Z-6 Kaus (Screech Owl) I fitted with a Ju 88C solid nose section, plus several Do 17Z-10 Kaus IIs. The designation Kaus identified aircraft as carrying the Rohr infra-red sighting device known as 'Spanner', which was intended to enhance the pilot's night detection of targets by reflecting the light from bomber exhausts. It was only partially successful, and was soon dropped from frontline aircraft.

Fathers of the force – Hauptmann Wermer Streib (left) took over command of NJG 1 and went on to score 65 victories. Falck (right) was quickly elevated to a command position, where he had no opportunity to improve on his seven kills achieved as a *Zerstörer* pilot in the early war campaigns (*Falck*)

The original II./NJG 1 which became III. *Gruppe* had been equipped with the Bf 109, single-seaters being officially regarded as useful night fighters throughout the conflict. It was, incidentally, a Bf 109 that is generally credited with achieving the first Luftwaffe night fighter victory on 8/9 July 1940. Flying with IV.(N)/JG 2, Oberfeldwebel Paul Forster intercepted a Whitley V of No 10 Sqn caught by searchlights and shot it down into the sea off Heligoland. Forster stated that he merely happened to be in the right place at the right time, with no special equipment to assist his kill.

A Whitley V was also the first victim to fall to NJG 1. Flying a Bf 110 over the Ruhr on the night of July 20/21, Werner Streib spotted what he initially took to be another Bf 110. Having correctly identified the British bomber the German pilot closed to 300 yards, his Bordfunker (radio operator), Unteroffizier Lingen, keeping a close watch on the raider. Opting for a beam attack, Streib pressed to 250 yards before he was seen, whereupon the tail gunner of the Whitley sent a stream of Browning machine gun fire in his direction. Now there was no doubt. The Messerschmitt turned to starboard to position itself below and astern of the bomber and Streib opened fire with cannon and machine guns. Flames were observed from the Whitley's starboard engine and the crew were apparently seen to bale out as the aircraft dropped away. RAF records confirmed the loss of two Whitley Vs, one each from Nos 58 and 78 Sqns, on that particular night, but in both cases the entire crew perished.

The broad operational parameters under which the *Nachtjagd* was established would be modified to meet continuing commitments. Much would depend on what the enemy did, for a defensive force must perforce await developments. At the outset no set 'tours of duty' were established for night fighter crews, and in general, single enemy aircraft were left alone, night fighters not being scrambled unless there was a likelihood of intercepting multiple targets.

Gruppe establishment would vary at different times and for a variety of reasons, but it was stipulated that a minimum of 30 aircraft would be needed for a unit to operate effectively from a forward area – i.e.

Wolf Falck's personal Bf 110C in full NJG 1 markings in 1940. Coded 'G9+GA', Wk-Nr 3920 had his then-current score of seven kills marked on both fin sections in white bars and the early night fighter marking of a yellow rear fuselage band (*Falck*)

An 8.*Staffel* NJG 1 Bf 110C reveals salient details including an extended crew ladder (which was supposed to be retracted before flight, but was often left in the down position) the ventral D/F loop and, again, the rear fuselage yellow band with the *Staffel* letter applied (*Price*)

away from more elaborate servicing facilities. This point last lay at the heart of deployment plans for the Luftwaffe in general, fighter forces being provided with a support infrastructure to enable them to operate from a network of airfields – some of them only basically-equipped – all over Germany. And the entire *Nachtjagd* would move around constantly during the war years.

Positive identification of airborne targets was necessary at all times, and crews understood that only two categories of victory claim – destroyed or probable – would be allowed. 'Damaged' claims were not considered. For a kill to be confirmed, the target aircraft had to be seen to be (a) on fire or (b) to explode on impact with the ground. If night fighter crews observed fire, but no evidence of the bomber striking the ground or disintegrating, it would be categorised only as a probable.

A system similar to that introduced for the day fighter *Geschwader* was used to calculate the scores of individual *Nachtjagd* pilots, who would ultimately be recommended for the award of medals as they accumulated sufficient points. As an example, 500 points were

'Wolf' Falck receives relief for a 'sore throat' by receiving the award of the *Ritterkreuz* (Knight's Cross) in Berlin on 7 October 1940. Major von Brauchitsch, Reichsmarschall Göring's aid, does the honours for the founder of the *Nachtjagd* (*Falck*)

required for the award of the Iron Cross (First Class). This system did not, however, endure, being replaced by one based on the number of 'war flights' made by an individual, and his length of service in the *Staffel*. There was no automatic award for the destruction of a set number of aircraft, although it was generally considered that the value of a victory for a night fighter was three times that of a day fighter.

Night fighters would take off in virtually all weather conditions if multiple enemy bombers were detected, but in time it was realised that their efforts were pointless if there was thick fog or cloud that reduced the ceiling to less than 250 ft, if there was 10/10th overcast up to 20,000 ft and if visibility was reduced to less than 800 yards. Individual crews would not be penalised if they chose to brave the elements and attempt to get above the weather, where they could play a 'lone wolf' role, often with success.

Considerable help was provided to the airmen by searchlights, although the enthusiasm of the crews manning the batteries was occasionally counter-productive. They were instructed not to cone a bomber with more than six searchlights when working with night fighters, this number being considered adequate for a *Nachtjagd* crew to pick up their target, and more beams tended to blind both the attacker as well as the pilot and gunners in the target bomber. Inevitably, though, larger cones were formed due to the fact that the men on the ground all wished to share in the victory. In the far from unusual event of night fighters themselves being picked up by their own searchlights, an ample number of Very cartridges were carried. These would be fired to alert searchlight and gun crews that friendly aircraft were airborne in their sector.

The Luftwaffe C-in-C, with Gen Lorzer at his side, addresses officers of the *Nachtjagd* at the ceremony marking Falck's award in Berlin on 7 October 1940. The group includes pilots Falck (second from left), Groth, Makrocki, (unknown) and Streib. Despite his widely quoted belief that the Luftwaffe would never need a night fighter arm, Göring gave full backing to the force in its early, formative, months (*Falck*)

INTRUDERS

On 1 August 1940 the night fighter command structure was expanded to become *XII.Fliegerkorps*, a 'single function' command with Kammhuber, since promoted to the rank of Generalleutnant, with overall responsibility. The *Nachtjagd* was the subject of a Führer Directive on 22 August, this giving Kammhuber the highest priority on defence equipment, especially radar, but falling short of ensuring a similar priority on aircraft and personnel.

From the outset the *Nachtjagd* was intended to undertake an offensive as well as defensive role, and the former had been confirmed by the creation of I./NJG 2 specifically to fly the Ju 88C and Do 17/215 in the long-range intruder role. This new *Geschwader* was boosted that same month by the formation of a second *Gruppe*, and I./NJG 3 had also been raised from V.(Z)/LG 1. Thus the *Nachtjagd* had a strength of six *Gruppen* by the end of 1940.

Only pilots and aircrew who showed aptitude for night flying were transferred from the *Zerstörergruppen* – Falck knew full well that finding enemy aircraft at night could be frustrating and far from easy, particularly over industrial areas where the RAF's prime targets were located. Haze from factory chimneys tended to form its own well nigh impenetrable 'cloud layer', which dissipated the intensity of the searchlights and reduced visibility for aircrew. The noise of flak bursts, explosions on the ground and aircraft engines offered a further distraction to the task in hand. Crews had therefore to be very alert, particularly as it

Wearing the ever popular kapok-filled aircrew lifejacket, the pilot of Bf 110C 'C5+DT' of 9./NJG 3 climbs aboard his aircraft at the start of yet another mission. Although probably associated more with the early days of the *Nachtjagd*, the overall black finish prevailed until mid-1943 (*via Maesel*)

was all too easy for friendly fighters to stray over designated flak belts surrounding the plum targets.

But *Hellenachtjagd* (illuminated night fighting) appeared to be the most effective method of detecting enemy aircraft at that time, and co-operation with the flak batteries, cited according to the importance of targets within each Luftgau district, was generally good. Night fighters flew towards flak zones at heights below 10,000 ft, and once at the edge, they were strongly advised to break off, or proceed at their own risk, as the guns would open up as soon as the aircraft broke off. Some areas were entirely flak-defended, and therefore regarded as 'forbidden zones' for night fighters.

Few such restrictions attended the operations of the new I. *Gruppe* of NJG 2, which embarked on long-range night intruder operations against RAF bomber airfields in September 1940. Such sorties had the tactically-sound objective of destroying enemy bombers on the ground, or shooting them down en route to or from their targets. The night defence of the UK was at that time vested in a handful of Beaufighters, Blenheims and Defiants, and although the Ju 88 crews did not undertake sorties without careful planning, the danger from RAF night fighters and AA fire was reckoned to be minimal.

Crews of NJG 2 based at Gilze-Rijen generally went on daily stand-by for operations from 1700 hours. If RAF aircraft were detected crossing the German or Dutch coasts within the *Geschwader*'s area of coverage, a message was passed by the Feldwebel who acted as liaison officer with local flak units, and he also informed the *Gruppenkommandeur*, who in turn ordered his aircraft off to patrol in the area where British aerodromes were located.

In actual attacks on enemy aircraft over England at that period of the war, Ju 88 crews were able to close to within 50 yards in some cases, although fire was generally opened at 300 yards range. It was widely believed that the British ground defences would not fire at two aircraft close together for fear of hitting the friendly machine.

Blenheims and Hampdens were usually attacked from astern, but a head-on firing pass often yielded satisfactory results as the pilot and/or engines could be rapidly put out of action. The engines of the Blenheim were found to be, in the words of one crew member, 'as vulnerable as expected. There was negligible risk in attacking Blenheims at night, and I never experienced return fire from the lower rear quarter when attacking Hampdens. But in no circumstances would we attack a Wellington from the rear because of the tail turret guns. A beam or quarter attack was always used'.

Intruder crews soon became used to employing all available light sources when it came to finding their target airfields. There were few landmarks over a generally blacked-out Britain, but roads often yielded lights from traffic, particularly after rain. Trains also gave off some light from their smokestacks and trolley buses could identified by the flashes made by their overhead electric guide rails.

Among the men who had been enthusiastic members of the *Nachtjagd* from the earliest days was Ludwig Becker of II./NJG 1. His first victory was scored on 16/17 October, the victim being one of ten bombers lost to various causes from bombing and mining operations.

Throughout the war the Luftwaffe entertained downed crewmen from the 'other side', the *Nachtjagd* being no exception. At the officers' club at Arnhem in the summer of 1941 members of an RAF bomber crew, their wounds having been attended to, are entertained by Wolfgang Falck and his comrades (*Falck*)

Amongst the many ex-ZG 1 pilots and crewmen who joined the *Nachtjagd* was Paul Gildner, who had already scored four day victories. After transferring, he became acutely aware of the possibilities that nocturnal sorties offered the experienced Bf 110 pilot. Gildner was, however, not alone in realising the difficulty that even the most experienced night fighter crew might face in attempting to shoot down the British twin-engined bombers. As they were all appreciably slower than the Bf 110, types such as the Wellington presented the *Nachtjagd* crews with a target that they could very easily over-shoot, which often resulted in them losing their quarry altogether. The recommended method was to lower the flaps to match the target's speed immediately it appeared in the gunsight.

For their part the British bomber crews soon adopted the 'corkscrew' manoeuvre, which was often successful in eluding night fighters. Luftwaffe intelligence advised a 'cat and mouse' pursuit, crews encountering a weaving bomber being instructed to reduce speed and fly straight ahead, for sooner or later the target would again appear in front of the fighter. Successfully concluding this tactic in a confirmed kill depended on the skill of the German pilot in question, and the type of aircraft he was flying at the time.

Less experienced pilots who tried to follow a corkscrewing bomber's turns and changes of altitude invariably lost it. And there was a good chance of losing the bomber if it corkscrewed to the right, for if the pursuer was flying a Do 17 or Ju 88 in which the pilot occupied a left-hand seat, it would immediately be lost to view. This problem did not effect the tandem-seated Bf 110 crew to anywhere near the same extent, although this should be taken to imply that Messerschmitt crews never lost potential targets.

The dress uniform for Luftwaffe officers was amongst the smartest worn by air forces anywhere during the war. Helmut Lent exhibits the typical trappings of his rank of Hauptmann, plus medals including the rather rare arm shield awarded to veterans of the Narvik campaign. Lent was not only one of the most highly decorated pilots in the Luftwaffe (winning the Oak Leaves, Swords and Diamonds to the Knight's Cross he had received in August 1941), he also finished second in the final tally of night fighter aces with 113 kills, 102 of which were scored nocturnally. Like a number of other high scoring *Nachtjagd Experten*, Helmut Lent lost his life in a flying accident, rather than in combat. On 5 October 1944, whilst landing at Paderborn at the end of a routine operational flight, Lent's Ju 88 ('D5+AA') suffered an engine failure just as the pilot was on his final approach. The wallowing fighter touched a high-tension cable and crashed, and although Lent was pulled from the wreckage, he succumbed to his injuries two days later – his crew was also lost in the accident (*Price*)

By the late autumn of 1940 I./NJG 2 was perfecting its long-range intruder war over Britain, although the creation of an effective operational doctrine was only achieved at some cost to the *Gruppe* – on the night of 23/24 November the Ju 88C-4 carrying *Gruppenkommand-eur* Maj Karl Heyse and two crewmen went missing. No news of its fate was ever received, but the aircraft was believed to have gone down into the North Sea apparently following a combat with an RAF aircraft, although no such skirmish was officially recorded at the time, assuming that the machine in question was a bomber.

On the same night 3.*Staffel* suffered a similar loss when Feldwebel Kurt Schlicht and his crew failed to return from a sortie. They too were assumed lost when their Ju 88 went into the North Sea. Karl Hulshoff, *Staffelkapitän* of 3./NJG 2, took over as *Gruppenkommand-eur*, with his place being duly taken by Oberleutnant Ulrich Mayer.

To give an idea of the serviceability and crew availability of a typical *Staffel* of the intruder *Geschwader* at the end of 1940, the record of 1./NJG 2 at Gilze-Rijen on 1 December is revealing. With twelve crews and ten aircraft (five Ju 88C-2bs, four Ju 88C-4s and one Ju 88C-4b) on strength, the unit had three aircraft fully serviceable. Of the remainder, one was reserved for training flights, one was away at Bremen for compass damage repair and no less than five were in the Gilze workshops having varying degrees of airframe and engine trouble attended to.

Of the crews, three were immediately available, three were 'conditionally available', three were considered unavailable as they were still under training, one was on leave and two were sick. With each Ju 88C then carrying three men, this situation could obviously be changed fairly rapidly in order to meet an urgent operational commitment, but this focus on specific crewing up shows a preference in keeping men together whenever possible.

Although the normal inter-service co-operation – if not rivalry - between the flak arm and the rest of the Luftwaffe was sorely tested at times, it lasted throughout the war to the general detriment of the enemy. At the end of 1940 the introduction of aircraft to help protect the Reich during the hours of darkness appeared to be vindicated by relative figures showing that since its formation, the *Nachtjagd* had destroyed 42 enemy aircraft to the flak regiments' 30.

DEBUT OF THE 'HEAVIES'

Among the personnel transferring to the *Nachtjagd* from *Zerstörer* formations early in 1941 was Helmut Lent, who joined 6./NJG 1. Pilots of his calibre were urgently needed, as the RAF was raising the stakes in its bomber offensive. By March the Stirling and Halifax had flown their first sorties, their four engines giving much improved range, and the capability of carrying heavy bomb loads – in addition the Avro Manchester began operations in February.

Along with their greater payloads, these 'second generation' British bombers featured heavier armament in the form of mid-upper turrets. Although armed only with machine guns, these turrets nevertheless increased the risk to the attacking night fighter. Some bombers, notably the Stirling and Halifax, carried additional beam guns, but as

With a factory-designed nose section, the Do 17Z-10 had a far more streamlined appearance than the first rudimentary conversions which employed a Ju 88 nose. This example was part of the intruder force of NJG 2 in 1940-41 (*Lutz*)

numerous German fighter crews noted with some satisfaction, there was no general attempt to give the bombers protection in their most vulnerable spot – on the underside of the fuselage.

It became abundantly clear that inflicting heavy losses on RAF squadrons bombing Germany by night was a herculean task. Kammhuber set about finding a more positive method of positioning his night fighters nearer their potential targets, and to bring the enemy aircraft down in substantial numbers. This had not been possible on any scale with fighter crews seeking their targets by searchlight illumination, or even by relying on ground radar plots. *'Hellnachtjagd'*, or illuminated night fighting, left far too much to chance.

Kammhuber eventually established a network of night fighter 'boxes', each of which was controlled by ground radar and incorporating aircraft, flak and searchlights in an attempt to cover all the approach routes taken by enemy bombers heading for targets in Germany. The name 'Himmelbett' (Heavenly four-poster bed) was given to these boxes to indicate the four elements of defence each one incorporated. To RAF crews the *Himmelbett* chain was nicknamed the 'Kammhuber Line'.

The year 1941 was a momentous one for German war aims – in March the Afrika Korps began operations in the Western Desert, and a small Luftwaffe contingent was transferred to the theatre from Europe to provide air support. As the desert war expanded, so German air assets were proportionally strengthened, although there would be little night fighter activity until later in the year.

During the spring 4./NJG 2 received examples of the Do 215B-5, the night fighter-intruder version of the Do 215 bomber. These aircraft were incorporated into the *Geschwader*'s offensive against bomber airfields in the British Isles, and small numbers of Dorniers were subsequently added to the strength of I. and II./NJG 2, as well as I., III. and IV. NJG 1.

In June Hitler's invasion of the Soviet Union removed a large proportion of the day fighter and bomber *Gruppen* available to the Luftwaffe in the West, and the Eastern Front would later require its own night fighter coverage. Pilots of the bomber units committed to the early fighting in Russia included individuals who would subsequently win widespread fame at the controls of a night fighter, among them Heinrich Prinz zu Sayn-Wittgenstein. One of two hereditary princes to serve with the night fighter arm, he transferred after flying 150 sorties in the East to become *Staffelkapitän* of 9./NJG 2.

Pictured with the rank of Hauptmann, Heinrich zu Sayn-Wittgenstein was one of two princes who won fame as night fighter pilots. His untimely death in January 1944 saw the prince's impressive scoring run halted at 83 victories (*via Toliver*)

This marauding *schwarm* of 'Wolf' Falck's Bf 110 night fighter section from NJG 1 were photographed from the rear cockpit of the third machine in the formation. Falck himself was flying the lead aircraft with the individual code 'B', which was painted on in red and picked out with a white outline (*Falck*)

This period of the war saw the formation of the first two *Gruppen* of a new night fighter *Geschwader*, NJG 4. Originally drawing its personnel and aircraft from I./ZG 26, the link with the standard *Zerstörergeschwader* was maintained insofar as the night fighters reverted to day operations – under the ZG 26 designation – on the Eastern Front later in the year. A second formation of I./NJG 4 would be activated in 1942.

AIRBORNE RADAR

In July 1941 the Telefunken company began testing a new radar small enough to be installed in a night fighter. Known as FuG 212 *Lichtenstein BC*, this was the first German AI (Airborne Interception) set to see widespread use. It had a minimum range of 600 to 1000 ft, and a maximum range of two-and-a-half miles. It required three cathode ray tubes (CRTs, 'scopes' or 'screens') giving range, azimuth and elevation data, and was considered to be reliable – but crews were not at all happy that the necessary external aerial array cut 26 mph off the speed of the Bf 110. Also, the 450W power source was not high enough to show targets with sufficient clarity, particularly at low altitudes, where scopes would cloud over as a result of ground returns.

This meant that the Bordfunker experienced no little frustration in maintaining a proper balance in his tuning control whilst at the same time keeping track of what the three CRTs were telling him. The slightest evasive action on the part of the target aircraft was often enough to break the contact. The undeniable advantages of *Lichtenstein* took months to be fully appreciated and accepted by the crews who had to use it – indeed, there was widespread hostility towards the whole idea. Results would change this attitude, and reliability of the FuG 202 set would be improved, this and other German radars being the subject of a continuous development programme.

Joining the Ju 88s of NJG 2 in the Western Desert, NJG 3 operated the Bf 110 in-theatre for a period of eight months. Its aircraft retained the 'L1' codes of V.(Z)/*Lehrgeschwader* 1 (its original unit), before adopting the 'D5' code of NJG 3. This aircraft was assigned to Unteroffizier Strohecker, who stands in front of it (*Crow*)

Installation of *Lichtenstein* radar in night fighters – the first type converted being the Do 215B – was completed as soon as sets were available. When operational reports filtered back, crews who had resisted the new device came to appreciate that enemy bombers now became vulnerable throughout their time over Europe. They might evade searchlights and flak and fly beyond the range of a ground radar plot, but they now ran a constant and very real risk of being detected by a night fighter working independently with the minimum of control from the ground.

NORTH AFRICAN *NACHTJAGD*

In October 1941, having successfully carried out intruder attacks over British bomber bases for just over one year, I./NJG received an order that surprised every man in the unit – it was forthwith transferred to the Mediterranean. A Führer directive emphasising the propaganda value of enemy bombers being seen to fall over the homeland rather than distant British airfields where visual evidence of success was almost non-existent, could hardly be ignored. And while the withdrawal of NJG 2 from Europe may have represented a significant tactical error – one compounded by the fact that no similar unit was to replace it in harassing British bomber bases – it was also true that the *Gruppe* had already suffered significant losses, with over 100 pilots killed, wounded and missing.

More positively from the German viewpoint, I./NJG 2 now had a number of pilots with aerial victory claims running into double figures. They included Oberfeldwebel Wilhelm Beier with 14 claims and Leutnant Hans Hahn, Feldwebel Alfons Köster and Leutnant Peter Laufs with 11 kills each. From the opening phase of NJG 2's combat period had emerged Heinz Strüning, who would eventually score 56 kills, Paul Semrau with 46, Beier with 36 and Koster 29. This quartet of top *Experten*, all of whom were *Ritterkreuztrager*, would figure prominently in the overall claims list of the entire *Nachtjagd*. The grim price of conflict for the Luftwaffe meant that only Beier was destined to survive the war, however.

The crews of I./NJG 2 had little choice but to pack their bags and point their Ju 88s in the direction of North Africa, where they duly

The end result of a hard landing on an airfield in Tripoli for Bf 110 'L1+BH' of 1./NJG 3, flown by Oberfeldwebel Jacke. The reason for the crash was either combat or storm damage. Note the owl and crescent moon insignia of 1./LG 1 (*Crow*)

arrived to occupy Catania airfield in Sicily. Much of November and early December were spent establishing base and servicing facilities, and mounting 'theatre familiarisation' patrols. Ju 88 crews found that they were up against similar RAF opposition to that found over England, with their own aircraft remaining unchanged. The night intruder role continued to rely on radio communications and routine intelligence sources, radar sets not being supplied for their aircraft.

In November 5./NJG 2 gained a new *Staffelkapitän*, the imposingly-named Egmont Prinz zur Lippe-Weissenfeld. An Austrian who had been a *Zerstörer* pilot with II./ZG 76, Lippe-Weissenfeld joined the *Geschwader* which had then been under the command of Helmut Lent for less than a week.

By the second week of December the crews who manned the black-painted Ju 88s of I./NJG 2 had settled into their new surroundings, and on 13 December 1941 Oberfeldwebel Hermann Sommer claimed the unit's first night kill in the area, over Crete. This, Sommer's eighth victory, was a Beaufighter, an aircraft not previously encountered by crews of the German unit, and one which was engaged on much the same type of operation as their own. Two more 'Beaus' were claimed over Malta in December, plus a Blenheim and a Hurricane, to close out the unit's victory tally for 1940/41 at 148 enemy aircraft.

On the 19th NJG 2 escorted other Ju 88s making shipping attacks on a convoy approaching Malta. Hurricanes from No 126 Sqn intercepted the German aircraft and one fighter was shot down in the ensuing combat and its pilot killed. This aircraft was flown by Plt Off Edward 'Pete' Steele, who thus became the first American to die in the defence of Malta. The victory probably fell to NJG 2 *Experten* Leutnant Peter Laufs of 1.*Staffel* for his 12th victory, although a Hurricane was also claimed destroyed by a Bf 109F flown by the Kommodore of JG 53, 68-kill Major Günther Freiherr von Maltzahn.

The combat resulted in the loss of the Ju 88 flown by Lt Wilhelm Brauns, and not unusually exact details remain conjectural in that this may have been the Ju 88 that Plt Off Steele was last seen firing at. In their turn the Ju 88 crew was observed to be firing at the Hurricane as it went down. These first weeks had thus cost I./NJG 2 three aircraft, one from each *Staffeln*, on 19, 22 and 28 December.

In the uniform of a Hauptmann, Egmont zur Lippe-Weissenfeld was the other 'fighting prince' of the *Jagdwaffe*. Like his contemporary Sayn-Wittgenstein, he too was later killed in action, with his score at 51 (*Toliver*)

ELECTRONIC EYES

The gradual build up of the *Nachtjagd* since 1940 was proof not only of the importance the Germans attached to the night defence of their cities, but the total commitment of the British to bombing as an instrument of war. As of January 1942 the night fighter force had about 250 aircraft at its disposal, comprising mostly Bf 110s and Ju 88s.

On 22 February 1942 Air Chief Marshal Sir Arthur Harris took over leadership of Bomber Command. Under him, the RAF bomber offensive would take on a whole new dimension as plans were implemented to forge a new and far more effective striking force. Shortly before Harris took office, a directive outlining the policy of 'area bombing ' of German cities was officially accepted. It was the new C-in-C's unenviable task to ensure that it was carried out.

At that time there were 469 bombers available for operations, including a number of the new 'heavies' capable of delivering a far greater weight of bombs than the twin-engined types with which the command had begun operations. Offsetting this advantage, and coinciding with Harris's appointment, was the service introduction by the Germans of airborne radar – the one item of equipment that was to give his aircrews their most difficult challenge. *Lichtenstein BC*, fitted in the early models of the Bf 110F, was an adequate combination, but both carrier aircraft and its new electronic aid soon needed upgrading.

By installing the 1475 hp DB 605B engine in a marginally modified airframe, Messerschmitt created the Bf 110G – the first model specifically intended for the specialist night fighter role. Introduced onto the production line in June 1942, the Bf 110G initially suffered some

A finish more in keeping with European operations was the two shades of dark green upper surfaces with blue undersides. This was applied to Ju 88C intruders of NJG 2, and other units, to gradually replace the overall black night fighter finish early in 1943. Many short-lived paint schemes were tried out at unit level before a universal light grey/white finish was chosen for *Nachtjagd* aircraft later that year (*Creek*)

A helping hand to get into the bulky Luftwaffe flying suit was always welcome, as Wolf Falck and a colleague demonstrate. The suit had to be close-fitting for warmth, although the uniform jacket worn underneath made for some difficulties in this respect (*Falck*)

As ever, the Luftwaffe 'black men' – the armourers, radio technicians, airframe repair teams and other specialists – were an integral part of every *Nachtjagd* unit. Thorough servicing of the Bf 110's guns between sorties was a crucial factor in ensuring that each night fighter *Staffel* had adequate aircraft at top line serviceability (*Price*)

problems with in-flight engine fires, but these were soon rectified. Inevitably, the extra weight of the radar aerials and associated night fighter equipment had some detrimental effect on performance, as both the Bf 110G's engines also needed a pair of cumbersome 'double' exhaust pipes incorporating flame dampers. To compensate for the extra weight forward, the area of the twin rudders was increased with larger trim tabs being incorporated.

Turning to the *Nachtjagd*'s other main weapon, early Ju 88s used as night fighters did not carry radar, the first to do so on an 'as standard' basis being the C-6 series. Production Ju 88C-6b and C-6c night fighters powered by Jumo engines were equipped with FuG 202.

Among the men who saw exactly how radar could make the whole night interception business that much more profitable for the Germans was Hauptmann Ludwig Becker. An enthusiastic exponent of airborne radar from the start, Becker flew a Ju 88 with the kind of skill that convinced the most doubtful sceptic.

Lichtenstein sets were ultimately to be fitted to a variety of second-line aircraft, primarily to aid in the training of radar operators. These included the He 111, Siebel Si 204 and Fw 189. The term night fighter later became somewhat blurred, for it encompassed numerous combat sorties by an assortment of hitherto second-line aircraft engaged mainly on nocturnal ground attack work.

The night fighter force was expanded again in April-May 1942 by adding a second formation to II.*Gruppe* NJG 4. This had its origins in 5.*Staffel*, but was otherwise a completely new unit with fresh personnel who would fly mainly Bf 110s on operations. In May III./NJG 5 was activated, its personnel transferring from three *Staffeln* of NJG 1.

Harris himself had to fend off numerous attempts to dissipate his force into other operational areas, and in May 1942 he laid on a demonstration aimed at finally convincing the sceptics that well concentrated bombing could cause great destruction. Cologne was chosen as the target on the night of 30/31 May, and by scouring all groups at his disposal (including training units), Harris was able to send 1047 aircraft to attack the city. Even though less than this number actually bombed the target, the figure was nonetheless impressive – nothing like it had ever been achieved before, and it offered the Germans a grim portent of what was to come.

Reaction by the *Nachtjagd* to the Cologne raid was rigorous, and as well as four bombers actually being shot down over the city, a further proportion of the overall RAF loss figure of 41 aircraft was additionally attributable to night fighters. One big challenge the Germans faced on this occasion was the sheer speed and time-space compression of the operation, for Cologne saw the first use of a bomber stream.

Whereas before a large number of individual aircraft entered successive *Himmelbett* boxes en route to and from their targets, planning for the Cologne raid called for a highly concentrated mass of bombers to penetrate only the very minimum number of boxes. Each *Himmelbett* box could then handle up to six interceptions per hour, too few to be really effective against multiple targets. The actual bombing of Cologne during the first RAF 'thousand bomber raid' was drastically reduced in time to just 90 minutes.

Among the successful pilots on the night of the big Cologne raid were Oberleutnant Emil Woltersdorf and Leutnant Manfred Maurer of III./NJG 1, who claimed a Wellington and Hampden respectively – both bombers drawn from second line units. Despite the additional eight victories credited to pilots of II./NJG 1, crews realised that they might have destroyed more bombers under a more flexible GCI system. *Himmelbett* had not been designed to cope with a bomber stream.

As the RAF bomber offensive gradually increased in effectiveness despite all that the German defences were doing to prevent that happening, the process of standardisation on a predominantly four-engined force continued. In March 1942 the Avro Lancaster had made its operational debut, and in May the Whitley was withdrawn from bomber operations just as the de Havilland Mosquito made its first appearance. The use of Whitleys on the Cologne raid, and the subsequent attack on Essen, was the result of 'making up the numbers' with OTU aircraft.

It was during the night fighter response to the Essen attack on 2/3 June that Heinz-Wolgang Schnaufer began his meteoric career. The aircraft that had the dubious honour of becoming his initial victim is unconfirmed, but out of 195 sorties, four Wellingtons, one Halifax and a Lancaster – plus a Hampden on mining operations – were lost to unspecified causes. Any one of these could have been Schnaufer's first kill. On 25/26 August the RAF attacked Bremen and Hans-Joachim Jabs destroyed his first enemy aircraft at night when he claimed a Stirling. His victim was one of three such aircraft known to have been attacked by night fighters.

Also making his combat debut in June was Günther Bahr, another ex-*Zerstörer* pilot who had gained considerable combat experience on the Eastern Front before transferring to the night fighter arm, initially to serve with NJG 4.

Nothing so potentially damaging as the bomber stream that relentlessly pounded the cities of Germany was met over the desert wastes of North Africa, NJG 2 continuing to fight its individual war for the first seven months of 1942. The Ju 88 crews shot down a variety of enemy

This Bf 110 of 4./NJG 1 came to grief on the seashore at Bergen/Herdla, in Norway on 20 February 1942. Note the Staffel's distinctive national flags marking along the side of the cockpit canopy (*Maesel*)

aircraft ranging from Swordfish to Marylands, and including the odd 'heavy' such as the Halifax and Liberator, although the majority of their kill claims during this period were made against Wellingtons. The unit was active over Tobruk in June, but it was clear that for the Luftwaffe, the desert campaign was becoming a difficult and wasteful exercise, outnumbered as the Germans had always been in the area by ever-growing Allied strength. Night fighter victories by I./NJG 2 tailed off significantly during the autumn months, there being a final claim (the 184th victory for the unit) filed by Oberleutnant Schultz for a Wellington on 10 September 1942.

In Europe, June saw the Manchester retired from Bomber Command, its successor having by then made its mark. Dornier had continued night fighter development of its basic bomber design with the Do 217J-2, deliveries of which began in the early summer. Examples were taken on charge by *Gruppen* of NJG 1 and 2, although the main Dornier-equipped units were III./NJG 4 and NJG 3, all *Gruppen* of the latter converting. NJG 3 and NJG 4 continued to be the primary users of Dornier nightfighters in that both *Geschwader* were subsequently fully-equipped with the Do 217N-1, N-1/U3 and N-2 variants, the latter version being the last built specifically for the role. The Do 27N-1/U3 carried two or four MG 151/20 cannon in a dorsal *Schräge Musik* installation aft of the wing.

On 17 August 1942 the USAAF began bombing enemy targets in occupied Europe in daylight. At first the number of heavy bombers deployed by the Eighth Air Force was modest, and reaction to the raids was left almost entirely to the flak batteries. But these incursions, like those of the RAF, were not stopped, and fighters – any available fight-

A paint finish deemed more appropriate than black was eventually applied to the Ju 88s of NJG 2 in the Mediterranean, as shown by this view of 'R4+FM', a *4.Staffel* machine flown by an undisclosed *Experten* whose score appears on the fin, partially obscuring the swastika – a not uncommon occurrence on Ju 88s of this and other units (*Lutz*)

ers – would soon be seen as the most effective method of bringing them down.

Fighting other aircraft at night was for the most part even more impersonal than daylight combat. It has often been said by fighter pilots that their war was one of machine versus machine, with the 'human element' rarely given more than a passing thought. For many reasons it had to be like that. But there were times when the human factor could hardly be ignored.

One incident that happened to Egmont Prinz zur Lippe Weissenfeld of NJG 1 left a lasting impression;

'One my easier and relatively unexciting assignments as a fighter pilot was keeping an eye on stragglers returning from bombing missions over Germany during the summer of 1942. Cruising in my Bf 110, I sometimes found these stragglers, mainly Wellingtons, Whitleys and Stirlings, up to 100 miles away from the main stream.

'Besides disliking these types of mission for the routine they had become, I always felt a kind of pity for the defenceless, hapless, bomber crew trying to reach home in an aircraft often already shredded by flak and cannon fire, no match for my faster, better armed, '110.

'I'd often close in, examine the aircraft and simply fire a few rounds in their general direction. In some cases the bomber crew did not even pretend to counter my fire, but evacuated immediately. This suited me fine. Only if machine gun fire answered my initial rounds did I pursue the bomber. Perhaps my feelings and behaviour were somewhat unorthodox, but it allowed me to live with myself.

'It was precisely during one of these "routine" assignments (almost certainly the night of 27/28 August 1942 when 306 aircraft bombed Kassel) that I was to witness one of the most startling sights of my entire career. The night was quiet with a full moon above. I had been patrolling the southern flank of an area below the Ruhr Valley. Flashes from bursting bombs and exploding aircraft over the city of Kassel seemed close, although it was well over 100 miles away. Their mission completed, the large RAF bomber stream was now returning to England. The gunner behind me reported no sightings. Flying at cruising speed, we seemed alone in the vast emptiness.

'Suddenly, approaching at phenomenal speed, oxygen mask flapping and parachute harness intact, an airman fell straight through the heavens towards the earth below, barely missing the starboard wing of my fighter. For one split second I looked into the frightened man's face. Never will I forget the shocked and terrified expression I read there.

'Recovering after what seemed like hours, my baffled gunner and I scanned the skies and still there were no visual sightings, just the dark and quiet night. Enough for this evening. We had already shot

The compromise made between protective camouflage paint designed to hide the aircraft and national insignia to confirm its identity is clearly visible in this view of a *rotte* of Bf 110Cs of NJG 4. The machine in the background with ten victories marked was almost certainly flown by Stabsfeldwebel Reinhard Kollack, who ultimately scored 49 victories (*Price*)

A haul of 65 night victories (including 40 'heavies' and two Mosquitoes) was no mean achievement by Hauptmann Manfred Meurer, who saw action with both NJGs 1 and 5. He was killed in action on 21 January 1944 (*Toliver*)

down a Wellington sometime earlier. We landed. But the mystery airman made it safely to the ground ahead of us. His parachute had opened in the black night below. His heavily damaged bomber continued on its way home to England with one crew member less . . .'

Bomber Command reported the loss of 31 aircraft from this raid, including no less than 21 Wellingtons. Most of the casualties were attributed to night fighters. Hampdens, perhaps surprisingly, soldiered on in Bomber Command until September 1942, when they were dropped from the order of battle. That left the *Nachtjagd* five types to cope with – the Lancaster, Halifax, Stirling, Wellington and Mosquito. The latter three aircraft also flew support operations other than direct bomber sorties against German cities, leaving the Lancaster and Halifax with the lion's share of such attacks (the core of what came to be known in the RAF as the Main Force), and against which the vast majority of the *Nachtjagd's* interceptions were made.

Expansion of the *Nachtjagd* continued into the autumn of 1942 with the raising of a second, more permanent, formation of I./NJG 4 and the first *Gruppe* of NJG 5 in September. Two months later a fourth *Gruppe* was added to NJG 3, together with second and fourth *Gruppen* to swell the strength of NJG 5.

Extra strength was certainly needed – the main worry for the Germans was not so much the individual capabilities of the enemy aircraft waging the night war, but the ever increasing numbers being sent out. Successful crews knew full well that even on nights when they destroyed multiple targets, some of their colleagues (those with limited experience) would almost certainly have downed none at all.

What the German aircrews could not know was the effect their efforts had on enemy morale, or if the percentage of kills they claimed was higher than the RAF would continue to stand. In truth, bombing conditions and results varied too much for any pattern to emerge. The RAF could not damage targets obscured by cloud as well as those attacked in clear conditions, so a successful raid on a given Monday night might not be possible on the same scale until Thursday, or even later, because the prevailing weather was not ideal. Equally, *Nachtjagd* reaction to raids was for many reasons inconsistent in terms of the number of bombers shot down.

Despite a steady flow of intelligence reports via *Ultra*, agents in occupied countries and prisoner of war interrogations which kept them abreast of *Nachtjagd* strength, equipment and unit movements, the British, for their part, could hardly anticipate how effective the German reaction to a given bomber operation might be.

Enemy intruders had been active over the continent since the war started, but these had little adverse effect on the *Nachtjagd*. However, news of the outstanding performance of the Mosquito did give some impetus to the search for new and improved night fighters for the Luftwaffe. Heinkel proposed a new twin in the shape of the He 219. Delayed both by RLM vacillation over the limited 'single role' of the aircraft and the effects of Allied bombing, which destroyed engineering drawings at the parent factory at Rostock-Marienehe, the He 219 finally flew in prototype form on 15 November 1942.

Kammhuber was initially enthusiastic over the aircraft, dubbed

'Uhu' ('Owl'), although Milch showed preference for the Ju 188, an extensively modified airframe based on the Ju 88. In many ways the He 219 actually filled a gap already created by a number of unsuccessful twins, notably the Ar 240, Fw 187 and Me 210, any one of which might have undertaken a 'second generation' nightfighter role.

ITALIAN *CACCIA NOTTURNA*

Thought had also been given to improving night fighter defence of the industrial areas of northern Italy, which had been raided by the RAF since the Italian declaration of war on 10 June 1940. During August and September 1942 the first two Italian instructor crews were re-trained at Stuttgart and Lechfeld, their courses initially covering operation of the Do 17Z and then the Do 217.

Four Bf 110s were supplied to Italy for evaluation purposes pending the delivery of operational aircraft, which were ultimately confirmed as fifteen Dornier Do 217J-1s and J-2s with *Lichtenstein* radar. These subsequently arrived at Milan/Treviso to become part of Italy's small night fighter force, equipping 41° and 59° *Stormo*. These units primarily defended the major industrial cities of Milan, Genoa and Turin, but by all accounts they were relatively ineffective in terms of confirmed aerial victories. A Lancaster III of No 207 Sqn bombing the Cislago electrical transformer station was claimed destroyed on the night of 16-17 July 1943, Capitano Aramis Ammannato of 235 *Squadriglia* being credited with the sole victory for the Italian-manned Dorniers.

In November 1942 Hans-Joachim Jabs was transferred to IV./NJG

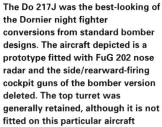

The Do 217J was the best-looking of the Dornier night fighter conversions from standard bomber designs. The aircraft depicted is a prototype fitted with FuG 202 nose radar and the side/rearward-firing cockpit guns of the bomber version deleted. The top turret was generally retained, although it is not fitted on this particular aircraft

Another view of the first Do 217J-1 as seen on the previous page. From this side-on angle the FuG 202 nose aerials and cannon armament set into the sloping forward fuselage can be clearly seen. The latter armament configuration proved to be extremely effective in combat, as underside guns reduced the risk of the night fighter pilot being blinded by the muzzle flash when he opened fire

1 (based at Leeuwarden in northern Holland), under the command of Helmut Lent, who had risen to the rank of Hauptmann. At that time the unit flew the Bf 110F-4 fitted with *Lichtenstein* C-1 radar, and Jabs continued his impressive scoring run. On 17/18 December he destroyed two four-engined bombers out of a force of 108 Lancasters, Stirlings and Wellingtons sent to attacked various German towns as well as the Opel Works at Fallersleben – with little success on this par-

The two top ranking fighter aces of the *Nachtjagd*, Oberleutnant Helmut Lent (left) and Hauptmann Heinz-Wolfgang Schnaufer are seen in discussion – between them, they destroyed a staggering 223 enemy aircraft. The photo predates October 1944, the month in which Lent was killed while he was Kommodore of NJG 3. Schnaufer was *Kommandeur* of IV./NJG 1 at the time (*Toliver*)

ticular occasion. The 18 aircraft that failed to return raised the night's percentage loss to a massive, but quite unrepresentative, 17.3 per cent.

There was a widespread feeling in the Luftwaffe – one not without foundation – that night fighting carried less risk to the crews involved than operating against the Allies by day. The statistics spoke for themselves, with the result was that not only were new pilots and crews joining the *Nachtjagd* in steadily increasing numbers, but experienced aircrew were requesting transfers. These were usually rubber-stamped by the authorities, as the activities of the enemy bomber force showed no sign of abating. And it was predictable that with the waning ability of the *Zerstörergeschwader* and *Kampfgeschwader* to survive combat operations in daylight without incurring heavy losses, many crews from both these branches of the Luftwaffe would make able night fighter crews following the minimum of retraining.

By the end of 1942 Hans-Heinz Augenstein had become a member of 7./NJG 1. Thus began a string of victories which would eventually lead to the award of the *Ritterkreuz* and command of 12.*Staffel*. Another eventual *Ritterkreuzträger*, Werner Baake, also joined NJG 1 in 1942, leading 3.*Staffel* for some time. He scored steadily against the RAF and eventually rose to become *Kommandeur* of I.*Gruppe* on 2 October 1944 – a position he was to hold until the end of the war.

In the meantime the early German success in Russia was meeting difficulties, not the least of which were very extended supply lines and a gradual deterioration in the weather. The Red Air Force remained active by night as well as day, and Prinz Sayn-Wittgenstein returned to the Eastern front in late August 1942 as *Kommandeur* of I./NJG 100. He stayed just five days, however, for his services were required back in the Reich at the head of II./NJG 3.

The unit the prince left behind in the east was just one of a number of *Nachtjagd* squadrons to see service over the Soviet Union, NJG 100 having been activated that August to fight a rather different war to the one facing units in the West. In the East it was not massed formations of bombers the Germans were up against, but 'low and slow' nocturnal 'nuisance' raiders. It was largely to combat these sorties, often flown by aircraft no more sophisticated than the Polikarpov Po-2 utility biplane, that part of the *Nachtjagd* was partially deployed in this theatre.

To guide their night fighters over a highly fluid frontline, the Germans packed ground radars (one *Freya* and two *Wurzburgs*) onto trains and sent them complete with operators to areas where it was believed that the Soviet intruders could be curtailed. While skilled personnel could unpack and assemble the radars for operation in six hours, electronic early warning did not generally prove to be anywhere near such an important asset in the USSR as it was in western Europe.

The term 'railway night fighting' nevertheless came to be used to identify the Luftwaffe's nocturnal war in the East, and among the successful pilots in that theatre was Alois Lechner. An ex-Lufthansa captain, bomber pilot and instructor, he joined NJG 100 and was subsequently credited with 43 victories on the Eastern Front, including seven kills in one night. Nine trains were ultimately allocated as mobile radar platforms, but NJG 100's Ju 88s tended to fight their war more as freelance agents rather than under close ground control.

Almost certainly an aircraft assigned to NJG 200, this Bf 110G, coded '8V', was photographed on the Eastern Front (*Lutz*)

1
Bf 110C (Wk-Nr 3920) 'G9+GA' of Major Wolfgang Falck, *Geschwaderkommodore* NJG 1, Arnhem, Autumn 1940

2
Bf 110C 'G9+AA' of Oberst Wolfgang Falck, *Geschwaderkommodore* NJG 1, Holland, June 1943

3
Bf 110G-4 'G9+AA' of Oberst Hans-Joachim Jabs, *Geschwaderkommodore* NJG 1, Lüneburg, May 1945

4
Bf 110G-4 'G9+AB' of Hauptmann Werner Streib, *Gruppenkommandeur* I./NJG 1, Venlo, March 1941

5
He 219 V9 'G9+FB' of Major Werner Streib, *Gruppenkommandeur* Stab./NJG 1, Venlo, June 1943

6
Bf 110C 'G9+HL' of Oberst Werner Streib, *Staffelkapitän* 2./NJG 1, Gütersloh, July 1940

7
Bf 110C 'G9+AC' of Hauptmann Walter Ehle, *Gruppenkommandeur* II./NJG 1, Arnhem-Deelen, October 1940

8
Bf 110E-2 'G9+BC' of Leutnant Gustav Ullenbeck, *Gruppen-Adjutant* II./NJG 1, Arnhem-Deelen, Spring 1941

9
Bf 110C 'G9+BM' of Oberfeldwebel Hans Rasper, 4./NJG 1, Bergen, November 1940

10
Bf 110C 'G9+LN' of Oberleutnant Heinz-Wolfgang Schnaufer, 5./NJG 1, St Trond, Summer 1942

11
Bf 110C 'G9+GP' of Leutnant Helmut Niklas, 6./NJG 1, St Trond, May 1942

12
Bf 110G-4 'G9+WD' of Oberleutnant Martin Drewes, *Gruppenkommandeur* III./NJG 1, Laon-Athies, March 1944

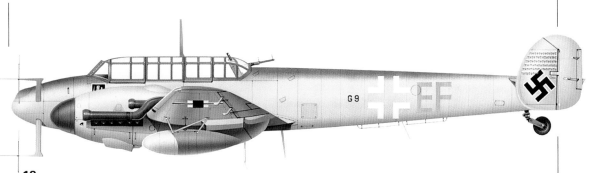

13
Bf 110G 'G9+EF' of Major Heinz-Wolfgang Schnaufer, *Gruppenkommandeur* IV./NJG 1, St Trond, October 1944

14
Bf 110G-4 'G9+EZ' of Oberleutnant Heinz-Wolfgang Schnaufer, *Staffelkapitän* 12./NJG 1, St Trond, February 1944

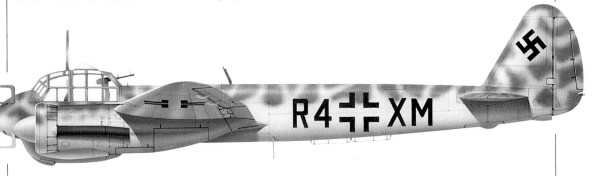

15
Ju 88C-6 'R4+XM' of Major Prinz Heinrich zu Sayn-Wittgenstein, *Geschwaderkommodore* NJG 2, Stendal, January 1944

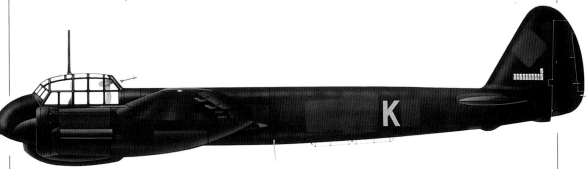

16
Ju 88C-2 'R4+KL' of Leutnant Alfons Köster, 1./NJG 2, Gilze-Rijen, October 1941

17
Do 17Z-10 'R4+AK' of Hauptmann Erich Jung, *Staffelkapitän* 2./NJG 2, Gilze-Rijen, Autumn 1940

18
Ju 88C-2 'R4+CK' of Leutnant Heinz Rökker, 2./NJG 2, Catania, 1942

19
Do 215B-5 'R4+DC' of Oberleutnant Helmut Lent, *Gruppenkommandeur* II./NJG 2, Leeuwarden, 1942

20
Ju 88C-6 'R4+AC' of Hauptmann Dr Horst Patuschka, *Gruppenkommandeur* II./NJG 2, Comiso, early 1943

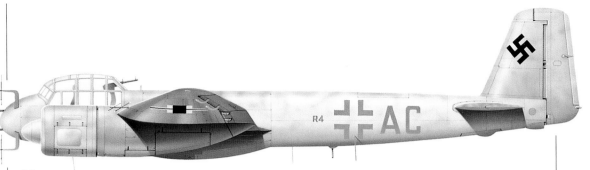

21
Ju 88G-1 'R4+AC' of Major Paul Semrau, *Gruppenkommandeur* II./NJG 2, Kassel-Rothwesten, Spring 1944

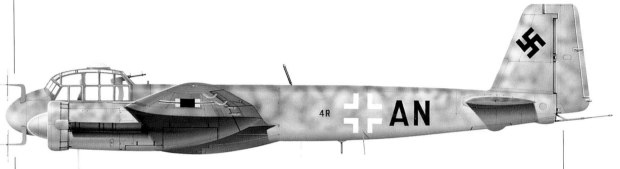

22
Ju 88G-6 '4R+AN' of Oberleutnant Erich Jung, 5./NJG 2, Mainz-Finthen, March 1945

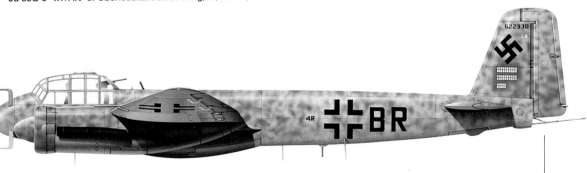

23
Ju 88G-6 (Wk-Nr 622330) '4R+BR' of Oberleutnant Walter Briegleb, *Staffelkapitän* 7./NJG 2, Kassel-Rothwesten, Autumn 1944

24
Bf 110C 'D5+AS' of Oberleutnant Walter Borchers, *Staffelkapitän* 8./NJG 3, Lüneburg, Winter 1941-42

25
Bf 110G-4 'G9+BA' of Major Heinz-Wolfgang Schnaufer, *Geschwaderkommodore* NJG 4, Schleswig, March 1945

26
Bf 110G '3C+MK' of Oberleutnant Martin Becker, 2./NJG 4, Florennes, Summer 1944

27
Bf 110F '3C+AR' of Oberleutnant Hans-Karl Kamp, *Staffelkapitän* 7./NJG 4, Mainz-Finthen, Summer 1942

28
Bf 110C '3C+LR' of Oberfeldwebel Reinhard Kollack, 7./NJG 4, Mainz-Finthen, Summer 1942

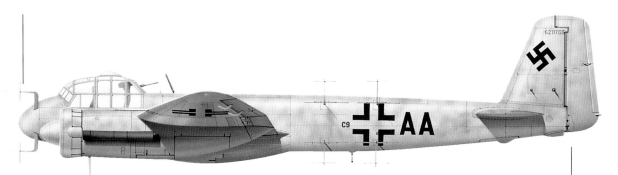

29
Ju 88G-6 'C9+AA' of Maj Rudolf Schoenert, *Geschwaderkommodore* NJG 5, location unknown, Spring 1945

30
Bf 110G-4 'C9+AC' of Oberleutnant Leopold Fellerer, *Gruppenkommandeur* II./NJG 5, Gütersloh, January 1944

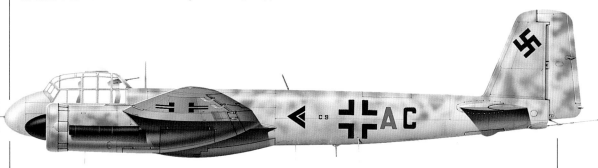

31
Ju 88G-6 'C9+AC' of Major Hans Leickhardt, *Gruppenkommandeur* II./NJG 5, Hagenau, late 1944

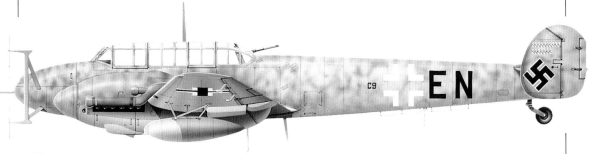

32
Bf 110G-4 'C9+EN' of Oberleutnant Wilhelm Johnen, *Staffelkapitän* of 5./NJG 5, Hagenau, April 1944

33
Bf 110G-4 'C9+AD' of Major Paul Zorner, *Gruppenkommandeur* III./NJG 5, location unknown, mid 1944

34
Bf 110G-4 'C9+AD' of Hauptmann Ulrich von Meien, *Gruppenkommandeur* III./NJG 5, Königsberg, winter 1944-45

35
Ju 88C-6 'C9+DE' of Hauptmann Prinz Heinrich zu Sayn-Wittgenstein, *Gruppenkommandeur* IV./NJG 5, Leipheim, early 1943

36
Ju 88G-6 'C9+AE' of Hauptmann Rudolf Altendorff, *Gruppenkommandeur* IV./NJG 5, Langensabza, Autumn 1944

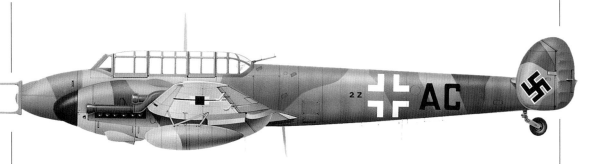

37
Bf 110G-2 '2Z+AC' of Hauptmann Rolf Leuchs, *Gruppenkommandeur* II./NJG 6, Echterdingen, March 1944

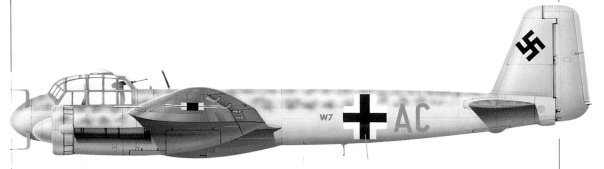

38
Ju 88G-6 'W7+AC' of Major Paul Zorner, *Gruppenkommandeur* II./NJG 100, Stubendorf, late 1944

39
Bf 109G-6 'Red 6' of Oberfeldwebel Arnold Döring, 2./JG 300, location unknown, August 1943

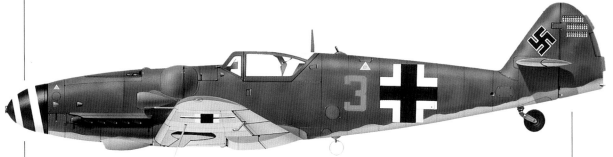

40
Bf 109G-14 'Green 3' of Major Friedrich-Karl Müller, *Gruppenkommandeur* of I./NJG 11, Werneuchen, late 1944

1
Hauptmann Heinrich Prinz zu
Sayn-Wittgenstein, *Gruppenkommandeur* of II./NJG 3 at Schleswig
in August 1943

2
Major Wolfgang Falck,
Geschwaderkommodore of NJG
1 at Arnhem in October 1940

3
Hauptmann Werner Streib,
Gruppenkommandeur of I./NJG 1
at Gilze-Rijen in the winter of
1941-42

4
Hauptmann Leopold Fellerer,
Gruppenkommandeur of II./NJG 5
at Leipheim in March 1944

5
Major Helmut Lent,
Geschwaderkommodore of
NJG 5 at Stade in August 1943

6
Oberleutnant Heinz-Wolfgang
Schnaufer, *Staffelkapitän* of
12./NJG 1 at Leeuwarden in
January 1944

HAMBURG WATERSHED

As 1943 opened, *Nachtjagd* strength had increased to 400 aircraft – 310 Bf 110s, 80 Ju 88s and 10 Do 217s. The majority of aircraft (150) remained in eastern France and Belgium, whilst 120 were based in Germany, 105 in Holland and the remainder in Denmark and Russia.

Unfortunately for the *Nachtjagd*, the waxing power of the USAAF heavy bomber offensive launched from Britain would have the effect of drawing in some night fighter crews to help boost the day fighters' attempts to blunt the American effort. Such operations risked the loss or incapacitation of trained crews in an operational arena in which their aircraft were extremely vulnerable, particularly to US escort fighters, which made their operational appearance in the spring of 1943. Any wasteful deployment of night fighters met with strong protestations from Kammhuber downwards, and these complaints were basically successful in preventing the *Nachtjagd* from being decimated.

However, among the crews sacrificed in this senseless way was that of *Ritterkreuzträger* Ludwig Becker. He and his radio operator, Oberfeldwebel Straub, were shot down into the North Sea on 26 February 1943 after having been ordered to intercept B-17s and B-24s attacking Wilhelmshaven. Out of Becker s total of 46 night victories, Straub had participated in 40 of them. At the time of his death, Becker was *Staffelkapitän* of 12./NJG 1.

Becker's death compounded NJG 1's loss of *Ritterkreuzträger* Paul Gildner just two days earlier, the 48-victory *Experte* having suffered an

Right
Delivered' to RAF Dyce in May 1943, Ju 88R-1 Wk-Nr 360043 of 10./NJG 3 still exists today as part of the RAF Museum collection at Hendon. The top photograph shows the aircraft being towed into a hangar immediately after landing in Scotland, whilst the bottom view focuses on the Ju 88's nose. Note the aerials of the FuG 202 *Lichtenstein BC*, the 7.9-mm machine gun barrels and the 'Englandblitz' badge below the cockpit (*Thomas and Price*)

Although not a production He 219, this aircraft (prototype V14) saw extensive use with Heinkel in a variety of development and test roles. It is seen here fitted with a BMW 003 axial-flow turbojet engine housed in a ventral centreline pod grafted on in place of the weapons tray. Development work carried out by this aircraft was instrumental in clearing the powerplant for use with Heinkel's He 162 Salamander – and may have solved the He 219's performance problems, had the aircraft been allowed to remain in production (*Aerospace*)

uncontrollable engine fire in his Bf 110 over Gilze-Rijen, causing him to crash onto the Dutch aerodrome whilst attempting to land.

German fortunes began showing a downward spiral of gradual setback, if not defeat, on all war fronts as 1943 progressed, nowhere more so than in the Middle East. NJG 2, now with two *Gruppen* in-theatre, was nevertheless about to be pulled back to Germany. One of the few victories achieved by the Ju 88s at that time was a Wellington on 19 April, shot down by Lt Heinz Rökker, who had subsequently been transferred to II. *Gruppe* – the stricken bomber ditched in the Gulf of Gabes. Earlier that same day Oberleutnant Machet of II./NJG 2 had shot down two Wellingtons, and this trio of bombers represented almost the final victories for NJG 2 in the Mediterranean, and they all but brought to a close the unit's detachment in North Africa. By the time the campaign ended in total defeat for the Axis on 13 May 1943, the small force of NJG 2's night fighters had achieved a combined total of 39 victories in the desert.

Returning once more to western Europe, the RAF, as well as regularly deploying a burgeoning force of heavy bombers, was stepping up its efforts to destroy German night fighters before they could even get close to their targets. Intruder sorties, hitherto flown by aircraft without radar, were given substantial help in June 1943 when No 141 Sqn

The following account of the defection of Ju 88R-1 (Wk-Nr 360043) 'D5+EV' to Scotland appeared in the December 1975 issue of *Air International*;

'Some mystery surrounds the acquisition by the Allies of the first night fighting Ju 88 which landed at Dyce, near Aberdeen, on the afternoon of Sunday, 9 May 1943. According to Royal Observer Corps records, the aircraft, a Ju 88R-1 of 10./NJG 3, would seem to have been expected as, after making landfall some 15 miles (24 km) north of Aberdeen, it was met by Spitfires which escorted the German fighter into Dyce.

'Last year, the Federal German popular newspaper *BILD AM SONNTAG* published an intriguing account of what it purports to be the true background. It alleges that the pilot, one Oberleutnant Heinrich Schmitt, son of the secretary to the then Minister for Foreign Affairs, Gustav Stresemann, had been an enemy agent since 1940, and had regularly supplied secret information to Britain through his father, who sent it from his home in Thüringen, via relay stations in Switzerland and Portugal.

'The flight of the Ju 88R-1 to Dyce had begun from the airfield at Christiansand, Norway. While still within range of German radio stations, Schmitt announced that he had an engine fire and would have to ditch, and then jettisoned three life rafts. The radio station that received the emergency call marked the spot in *Planquadrat* (area) 88/41 from which it had been transmitted, and assuming that the aircraft had gone into the sea when no further message was received, activated the search and rescue procedures.

'The aircraft was presumed lost, which was precisely what Schmitt and his crew, Oberfeldwebels Paul Rosenberger and Erich Kantwill, had intended. The aircraft then flew directly to the Scottish coastline, picked up its escort of Spitfires and then flew to Dyce, where, after landing, it was immediately surrounded by military police who had cleared the area of casual observers. The Ju 88R-1 was fitted with FuG 202 *Lichtenstein BC* which was promptly evaluated, and the successful conclusion of the defection was signalled to Schmitt's father via the British secret radio station *Gustav Siegfried eins*, the code phrase being "*der Mai ist gekommen*" (May has come). The Luftwaffe was to learn of the desertion in the following month when both Schmitt and Rosenberger broadcast over British radio'

Heinz Rökker enjoyed early success with the intruder unit NJG 2. His score eventually reached 64, all but one of his kills being claimed at night (*Toliver*)

Kurt Tank's *Moskito-Jäger*, the Ta 154. A pleasing design incorporating much of the latest thinking on warplane configuration, including a tricycle landing gear, the aircraft was hamstrung by the poor bonding of its wooden components. It was operationally tested in small numbers by a few units including NJGr 10 (*MAP*)

initiated the first sorties with Beaufighters fitted with AI Mk VI radar, the navaid *Gee* and the *Serrate* homing device. Despite many sorties by this and other units, the Beaufighter did not prove a particularly lethal aircraft to the *Nachtjagd* due to its temperamental electronic aids. What followed later in the year in the shape of the Mosquito was a different story, however – the need for a German night fighter able to match the de Havilland twin became acute.

With initial flight testing behind it, the He 219 had made progress during the winter, benefiting from the combat experience of Werner Streib, by then *Kommandeur* of I.*Gruppe* NJG 1. Seconded to Heinkel as an advisor, Streib's enthusiasm for the He 219 helped the programme along. A boost of an entirely different and unexpected kind occurred in late January when Mosquitos attacked Berlin, their appearance timed deliberately to interrupt speeches by Göring and Goebbels.

The Nazi hierarchy then knew what the *Nachtjagd* had been aware of for months – the Mosquito was proving extremely difficult to intercept. Calls went out from the highest levels for a *Moskito-Jäger* (Mosquito-hunter) to equip the *Nachtjagd* without further delay.

Delays continued, however. Kurt Tank muddied the waters by making a convincing case for a German equivalent of the Mosquito with his Ta 154 interceptor, which would be economically attractive to Berlin through its extensive use of wooden construction for lightness and speed. Milch, still backing the Ju 188, recommended cancellation of the He 219, and Heinkel realised that his own case could only be strengthened by proof that his new night fighter could do the job it had been designed for – Streib was ordered to lead a *Gruppenstab* section within I./NJG 1 at Venlo to test the He 219 in combat.

Since early 1943 the German night fighter force had become almost completely dependent on radar for its defence of the Reich operations. From being viewed as a difficult to use 'new fangled' additional work-

load for crewmen, it had matured remarkably quickly into a vital aid to nocturnal interception. By mid-1943 Germany was covered by the elaborate *Himmelbett* early-warning system, comprising sites with *Freya*, *Wurzburg* and *Giant Wurzburg* radars. Improvements in direction finding accuracy had been utilised by Kammhuber to develop his system to the point of such tight control that it was forbidden for a night fighter to fly any form of defensive sortie other than under *Himmelbett* direction. This rigidity was about to be sorely tested.

Streib was able to see what the He 219 was capable of on the night of 11/12 June when a Bomber Command 'maximum effort' sent 693 aircraft to Dusseldorf, the city being marked by Oboe-equipped Mosquitos. Guided to multiple targets by his Bordfunker, Unteroffizier Fischer, Streib expertly handled the Heinkel fighter and shot down five bombers, a remarkable achievement for a new and untried aircraft. Two of Streib's victims were identified as a Halifax II of No 78 Sqn and a Lancaster II of No 115 Sqn. NJG 1 had other successes that night too, single Halifaxes from Nos 35 and 77 Sqns falling to Hauptmann Eckart-Wilhelm von Bonin of 6.*Staffel*, a Stirling of No 75 Sqn going to Oberleutnant Wilhelm Telge of Stab II.*Gruppe* and a Wellington of No 429 Sqn to Leutnant Werner Baake of I.*Gruppe*.

Returning to Venlo, Streib made a normal approach, selecting flaps down. When the lever failed to lock, the flaps promptly retracted and Streib had a crisis on his hands as the sleek night fighter went out of control. When the starboard engine seized, it broke away from the wing as the aircraft hit the runway, the impact severing the cockpit section and break-

Poor quality, but nonetheless interesting, view of a He 219, the black underside to its starboard wing offering an instant recognition aid for friendly flak gunners – a continual problem for the *Nachtjagd* throughout the war. The degree of exhaust deposit visible from the port engine also highlights another of the He 219's major problems – powerplants that were too persistently unreliable to allow the Heinkel to operate as an effective nocturnal fighter. This particular He 219, coded 'G9+FK', was the mount of Hauptmann Ernst-Wilhelm Modrow of 2./NJG 1, who scored 33 victories

ing the machine's back. Streib and Fischer, still strapped in their seats, rode their truncated 'vehicle', with the nosewheel attached, down the runway, before finally coming to rest on their side about 150 ft away from the main wreckage. Neither man could quite believe he had survived, let alone avoided serious injury.

The dramatic end to Streib's combat debut in the He 219 did not detract from the new type's potential, and for some ten days afterwards the Heinkel fighter was used in action by other NJG 1 crews. The result was the destruction of about 20 RAF aircraft.

In view of the close proximity of the propellers to the He 219's cockpit, some doubts had originally been voiced over the crew's chances of a safe bale out in the event of an emergency, a problem anticipated by Heinkel, who had incorporated the world's first ejector seats into the design. Some RLM officials also distrusted the tricycle undercarriage, although this presented few problems on operations.

Despite the promise of new aircraft, the bulk of the *Nachtjagd* continued to rely on the Bf 110 and Ju 88. Further expansion took place

The end of an effective night's combat for Werner Streib on 11/12 June 1943. His first operational sortie in the He 219 had ended like this when the aircraft suffered a catastrophic engine failure and crash landing, which both pilot and radar operator were lucky to survive without injury. The double chevron denoting Streib's rank of major is just visible on the remains of G9+FB's fuselage

Airborne radar in the form of FuG 202 *Lichtenstein BC* transformed the *Nachtjagd*, largely freeing it from restrictive ground control, which had been designed to track individual bombers rather than the streams introduced by the RAF in May 1942. This Bf 110F-4 of 4./NJG 1 is undergoing a fairly full service in order to make it ready for the forthcoming night's work. Note the designator letter for the DB 601N engine on the forward cowling (*Price*)

in August 1943 with the activation of I./NJG 6. This *Geschwader* had had a IV. *Gruppe* since May and a V. *Gruppe* had been in existence for a few weeks in June, before becoming III./NJG 2.

Notwithstanding continuing criticism from Milch, Heinkel initiated production of the initial batches of He 219s, the A-0 being superseded by the He 219A-5 – unbuilt projects took up the intervening suffix numbers. There followed the improved He 219A-6 and A-7.

Werner Streib was promoted to *Geschwaderkommodore* of NJG 1 on 1 July, his place at the head of I. *Gruppe* being taken by Hauptmann Hans-Dieter Frank. With a string of victories to his name, Frank was well qualified to lead the first *Gruppe* of the premier night fighter unit. The first few months of 1943 had seen this and other units shooting down enemy bombers in substantial numbers, some being destroyed with consummate ease in a very short space of time.

If those on the ground saw scant little evidence that enemy raids were being rendered less effective by the defences, they might have been temporarily encouraged by the following figures – to drop 57,000 tons of bombs on German targets in the period 5/6 March to 24 July 1943, Harris had lost 1000 aircraft. And although this represented only 4.3 per cent of the total 23,401 sorties flown, the rising cost of the campaign gave cause for concern. Harris was therefore relieved, as he prepared to top off the recent round of Ruhr raids with an attack on Hamburg, to be given the all clear to make initial use of a simple aid that promised his bombers a significant degree of protection.

When the Hamburg raid was launched on the night of 24/25 July, with 791 aircraft flying towards the city and port in clear conditions, the force might have appeared highly vulnerable to fighter and flak defences. But as the German night fighters were scrambled and their Bordfunkeren tuned in their radar screens, chaos ensued. The screens were suddenly snowed out – thousands of aircraft seemed to be in the air, an enormous force creating a blizzard of echoes. It became almost impossible for the crews to pick individual targets.

In reality German radars were being blinded by an 'electronic storm' of false echoes created by 'Window' – tinfoil strips 27 cm long and 2 cm wide, which exactly matched half the wavelength of the *Wurzburg* and *Lichtenstein* radars. Just how effective 'Window' was on its initial use was shown by the

A Bf 110G with the early
Lichtenstein radar array that cut
about 25 miles per hour off the ideal
intercept speed. Crews who thought
that was bad had a shock in store as
the 'stag's antlers' required by the
SN 2 set had yet to appear! Drag
from the aerials turned out not to be
as detrimental to the Bf 110's
performance as many had predicted

losses of RAF bombers that night – only 12 failed to return. Of these, NJG 3 got two Halifaxes (of Nos 51 and 158 Sqns) and a Stirling (No 75 Sqn), while IV./ NJG I downed two Lancasters from No 103 Sqn.

Both sides were aware of the effects that 'Window' had on radar, and neither had risked using it in action for fear of a reprisal in kind – German scientists had even been forbidden to continue experimental work on what they termed *Duppel* (after the name of the estate over which it was first tested) for fear of its secret being leaked. But by the time of the four Hamburg raids, the initiative for bomber support techniques had passed almost entirely to the British. The Luftwaffe's own bombing effort had never even approached the mid-1943 scale of devastation now being meted out on German cities, and there was little fear that anything similar could now be visited upon Britain. Unfortunately for the people of Hamburg it began a chain reaction that tore the heart out of their ancient city on the River Elbe.

'Window' had a far-reaching effect on the German night fighter force. It was quickly realised that the carefully planned *Himmelbett* system would have to be circumvented – clearly, the fighter direction boxes appeared to have been rendered virtually obsolete in a single night. That was not quite the case, however, for the Germans found that 'Window' clouds, once recognised for what they were, could be turned to their advantage. Obsessive secrecy over the problem hardly helped the process of finding an answer, but within about ten days of the Hamburg raid an interim solution was found.

As far as *Wurzburg* was concerned *Wurzlaus*, which relied on the Doppler effect, appeared able to restore some guidance capability, but time was needed to fully verify the results. Real success was only possible if all German radars could be provided with the facility to change frequencies rapidly. From seemingly being an exclusive aid to the enemy, night fighter crews learned to use mass 'Window' returns to actually locate the bomber stream.

Some drastic reorganisation of the *Nachtjagd* was nevertheless deemed necessary, as the twin-engined types that formed the core of the force now faced a potentially enormous disruption to both their airborne interception capability and ground control. Little time was lost in introducing a number of temporary solutions independent of the discredited *Himmelbett* system, and these set the pattern for German night fighting until war's end. The process of change included the introduction of a form of night interception that was a variation on an old theme – '*Wilde Sau*' (Wild Boar).

Kammhuber was relieved of overall control of the *Nachtjagd*, three new commands being created instead. Of these, *I.Jagdkorps* was the largest, reporting directly to *Luftflotte Mitte*, which was specifically established to direct the defence of Germany. Generalleutnant Josef Schmid, named as the new CO, effectively stepped into Kammhuber's shoes, although the shake-up did not spell the end of the career of the man who had built the *Nachtjagd* up from scratch.

'*Wilde Sau*' was brought to fruition by experienced bomber pilot Oberst Hajo Herrman who, with Göring's backing, established a separate command alongside *XII.Fliegerkorps* and authorised the raising of three new units – JG 300, 301 and 302 – to fly Bf 109s and Fw 190s at night. Lacking radar that could be jammed, these fighters would operate on a freelance basis. To direct the pilots, the reportage system was employed, a running commentary being broadcast over several frequencies reserved for the '*Wilde Sau*' force.

Operating primarily as *Objektnachtjagd* (target area night fighters), the '*Wilde Sau*' pilots sought out bombers silhouetted against the glow

Single-seat fighters started Luftwaffe night fighting – and they probably would have ended it, had it not been for improved radar that revived the conventional force. Hajo Herrmann's '*Wilde Sau*' fighters nevertheless filled a significant gap with Bf 109s and Fw 190s, although the work was hazardous in the extreme. In this propaganda photo these Bf 109Fs appear to be day fighters 'borrowed' for the night s work – typical of early '*Wilde Sau*' operations, in fact. Note the kill bars on the fighter's rudder

from the fires of bombed cities. Even when an area was covered by cloud or smoke, searchlights could also 'project' the shadow of bombers into the overcast. This cloud illumination was colloquially known as 'shroud procedure' amongst the pilots, and *'Wilde Sau'* effectively filled the gap created by the problems now facing conventional night fighters. The downside was that the single-engined pilots often ran the gauntlet of free-firing flak in the bombers' target area.

To reduce casualties from their own flak, and undertake '*Wilde Sau*' night fighting sorties on a more organised basis, 1/NJGr 10 intensively tested Bf 109s and Fw 190s fitted with FuG 217 *Neptun* radar. This Fw 190A-9/R11 was the end result of the evaluation, the tailplane of the machine (Wk-Nr 550148) being used as a handy 'table' on which Oberleutnant Hans Krause can sort out his flying gear prior to strapping in. One of the more successful pilots within 1./NJG 10, based at Wernuechen, Krause gained 28 victories and was awarded the *Ritterkruez* on 7 February 1945. He ended the war with the rank of Hauptmann (*Lutz*)

At first only a single *Gruppe* of JG 300 was organised with its own aircraft – in order to get the '*Wilde Sau*' force operational in the shortest possible time, the remainder were '*Aufsitzergruppen*' with no aircraft of their own. Pilots were authorised to 'borrow' standard day fighters for their nightly forays, a policy that had obvious flaws. Feelings duly ran high when day fighter pilots found their aircraft either unserviceable as a result of damage at the hands of their night flying brethren, or missing entirely as '*Wilde Sau*' casualties increased. These reached the point where it was widely said that the great mass of '*Wilde Sau*' pilots had more parachute jumps on their records than kills!

Fitting radar in single-seat fighters was one answer to the loose approach to freelance night fighting adopted by Herrman, and a programme was initiated to perfect the installation of the *Neptun* set in the Bf 109 and Fw 190. The latter type soon gained preference due to its heavier armament, and the fact that any extra weight tended to have a detrimental effect on the lighter Bf 109's handling characteristics.

Operationally, examples of the Fw 190A-5, A-6, A-8 and A-9 saw service as radar night fighters, primarily with NJG 11, whilst examples were also flown by III./NJG 1 and IV./NJG 3, as well as a number of smaller formations. The leading *Experten* on the Fw 190 emerged as casualties rose, depriving the regular *Nachtjagd* of some of its best pilots like Hauptmann Köster of NJG 2, who was killed in action on 7 May 1943. With his score at 29, Köster had been one of the original *Experten* of NJG 2, which had recently returned from the Middle East.

At the end of July the Ju 88s of III./KG 3 were withdrawn from the Eastern Front to Munster Handorf, and the component 9.*Staffel*, having previously tried out flare-dropping sorties, went over to freelance night fighter patrols. This activity pointed the way to a future for the personnel of a number of *Kampfgeschwader* whose operations were being increasingly curtailed by Allied strength – conventional Luftwaffe bomber units, like the *Zerstörergeschwader* before them, were losing their usefulness, and indeed their ability to survive without prohibitive losses in both crews and aircraft. Transfer to the night fighter force proved to be both economical and practical, for trained bomber crews encompassed pilots, navigators and gunners, all of whom were included in a typical night fighter crew.

Fw 190A-5s intended for night fighting boasted limited flame-damping for the BMW engine and somewhat cumbersome Yagi aerials under the wings. The radar system worked well enough in combat (*Lutz*)

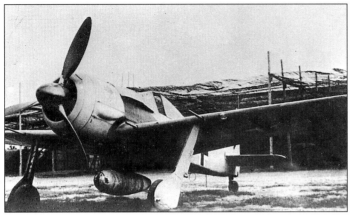

Another shot of 'White 11' flown by Oberleutnant Krause, this time showing the exhaust glare shield and the three rod aerials in front of the windscreen required by the *Neptun* radar system (*Lutz*)

Behind the scenes Erhard Milch was still trying to provide the *Nachtjagd* with new aircraft, but his misguided methods bore little fruit. He finally succeeded in persuading the RLM to cancel the He 219, arguably one of the best aircraft for the night interception role had it been possible to carry out a much more rigorous test and development programme.

Heinkel had little choice but to accept the official decision, although he complied only slowly to an order which was not unique to his firm. The deliberations of the *Jägerstab* would result in the cancellation of numerous types then under development so that industry could concentrate resources on single-engined day fighters and jet aircraft. Heinkel therefore built just 268 He 219s, including prototypes.

Among the *Nachtjagd* casualties in September 1943 was Hans-Dieter Frank, *Kommandeur* of I.*Gruppe* NJG 1 since 1 July. Promoted to major, Frank had become a *Ritterkrauzträger* in June and was subsequently lost in a collision with a Bf 110 during an interception over Hanover on 27 September while flying a He 219A-0 – a handful of Heinkel fighters had been declared operational in NJG 1.

In an effort to overcome the effects of 'Window', the Germans introduced the *Lichtenstein* SN-2 radar, which was indeed effective in giving the *Nachtjagd* back much of its artificial night vision. Coupled with *Naxos*, which homed onto the RAF's H$_2$S radar, and *Flensburg* which gave much the same guidance by detecting transmissions from the bombers' 'Monica' IFF sets, the German night fighters regained the initiative they had temporarily lost over Hamburg in July.

Although He 219 deliveries had increased, poor serviceability of its radar regularly obliged crews to revert to the trusty Bf 110s – few wanted to fly an aircraft with equipment that might let them down at the critical point of interception, particularly when the enemy was attempting to neutralise German radar. Engines of less than the required performance also continued to hamper the He 219. Bf 110Gs and Ju 88Gs also filled gaps left in the *Nachtjagd* inventory by the slow delivery rate of the Dornier Do 217N at this time, although NJG 5 and NJG 6 had received numerous examples.

Seasonal bad weather in late 1943 affected both defenders and attackers alike. Cloud covered potential Bomber Command targets on numerous occasions, and as a result the concentration of high explosives, despite the widespread use of Pathfinders using sky markers, varied significantly. The RAF had dropped the Stirling as a frontline bomber in September (Wellingtons also went in October), and this effectively removed about 250 aircraft from the order of battle at a critical time, for Harris was about to launch a highly ambitious campaign. On 18/19 November the RAF began an assault on the German capital. What later became known as the 'Battle of Berlin' would last into the following spring, and encompass 16 raids on the city.

Unusual plan view of a Do 217N in night black finish. The result of a lengthy development programme, the type served the *Nachtjagd* as both a frontline aircraft and a crew trainer. The small Italian night fighter force also used Do 217s as frontline equipment (*Price*)

This close-up shot shows the complex arrangement of FuG 202 aerials, four MG 151 20 mm cannon barrels (fitted with flash suppressors) below the antennae and four MG 17 machine guns above which crowded the nose section of the Do 217N-2. This combination made the converted Dornier bomber a formidable opponent once it started appearing in the night skies over occupied Europe during the winter of 1942/43 (*Aerospace*)

The bombers flying these hazardous, long-range, sorties represented the game in a fertile hunting ground for the '*Wilde Sau*' fighters, but at considerable cost to themselves. Bad weather was responsible for a proportion of the German casualties – reliably quoted as reaching 1000 by war's end – from units engaged in this method of night fighting.

Not all pilots who wished transition from day to night operations found the switch easy. One such individual was Fritz Lau who, despite having flown Ju 52/3ms in the Polish campaign before becoming an instructor, was repeatedly turned down. He finally succeeded in joining 9./NJG 1 and scored his first night kill in late 1943. His perseverance to affect a transfer was rewarded by elevation to *Staffelkapitän* of 4./NJG 1 in 1944. Lau was later made a *Ritterkreuzträger* in April 1945, having destroyed 27 bombers and one Mosquito.

Among the RAF pilots who did their bit to deprive the *Nachtjagd* of some of its top aces was Wg Cdr Bob Braham of No 141 Sqn. On the night of 29/30 September he finished a tour on Beaufighter VIFs with a final kill (his 20th out of a total of 29). His victim was 53-victory *Experte* Hauptmann August Geiger of NJG 1. Hit by the British fighter's fire, Gieger baled out of his Bf 110 over the Zuider Zee, but was

Having destroyed 53 enemy aircraft, August Geiger was finally shot down and killed by RAF night fighter ace, Wg Cdr Bob Braham, in a No 141 Sqn Beaufighter IVF on 29 September 1943 whilst flying Bf 110G-4 (Wk-Nr 5477) 'G9+ER' over the Zuider Zee. He was the second high-scoring *Experte* from NJG 1 to be killed in just 48 hours, 55-kill ace Hans-Dieter Frank having lost his life in a flying accident in He 219A-0 (Wk-Nr 190055) 'G9+CB' on the 27th (*Toliver*)

Gruppenkommandeur of I./NJG 4 from September to December 1944, Willi Herget was a leading night fighter *Experte* who scored 12 *Zerstörer* and 57 night kills, before transferring to a staff job and ending the war back on operations with JV 44. He flew an Me 262 fitted with a 50-mm cannon against American day bombers, an experience he somehow survived (see *Aircraft of the Aces 17 - German Jet Aces of World War 2* for more details) (*Toliver*)

Lined up for ease of servicing and crew boarding prior to take-off, only some of these Bf 110Gs have radar fitted, but all machines have the standard drop tanks plumbed in to restore any loss of range that the aircraft suffered by carrying extra weight. Only if the destruction of an enemy aircraft necessitated a long chase did the Bf 110 prove a little 'short-legged' (*Price*)

drowned when his parachute dragged him under. Braham had been the scourge of NJG 1 during 1943, having claimed *Experten* Oberfeldwebel Georg Kraft (14 kills) and Feldwebel Heinz Vinke (54 victories) in their Bf 110s on the same night on 17/18 August over Schiermanikoog-Ameland.

Apart from combat attrition, accidents steadily depleted the *Nachtjagd*, as did the unwelcome attention of German flak. Despite the previously agreed recognition signals, trigger-happy gunners claimed the lives of a crack night fighter crew on the night of 31 October. Returning from intercepting bombers over Munich, Hauptmann Rudolf Sigmund, and his two crew died when their Bf 110G was downed at Fassberg. Known as the *Viermotorenknacker* (four-engined bomber specialist), Sigmund had led III./NJG 3 from 31 August 1943, and had scored all but two of his 28 kills at night.

On the night of 20/21 December Bomber Command mounted a 650-strong raid on Frankfurt. German controllers plotted the route of the bomber stream early on and continued to monitor the force all the way to the target . Night fighters were sent up in force, and numerous combats ensued. Among the pilots in action was an *Experte* of modest stature, Willi 'Titch' Herget downing eight bombers in the space of 50 minutes. For one kill Herget latched onto a Lancaster and manoeuvred his Bf 110 with outstanding skill, stationing his aircraft below the bomber. Herget used its engine exhaust glow as an aiming point, carefully keeping station until he couldn't possibly miss. Four rounds left the barrels of his cannon. They were enough. The stricken Lancaster fell away.

'WILD BOAR' AND JAZZ MUSIK

On 1 January 1944 Prinz zu Sayn-Wittgenstein relinquished his position as *Kommandeur* of II./NJG 2 and transferred to the *Geschwader*'s *Stabschwarm*. Then with more than 70 victories, including 29 in Russia, this remarkable man had become 'virtually possessed' by the night fighting creed. Indeed, his tally was only bettered by Schnaufer and Lent.

Relatively few experienced *Nachtjagd* pilots succumbed to the generally poor defensive armament of the British bombers they attacked, but Paul Szameitat, 29-victory *Experte* and *Kommandeur* of I./NJG 3, was one. On 1/2 January he had attacked part of a substantial raid (421 Lancasters) on Berlin in his Ju 88C-6 (Wk-Nr 750444)'D5+EN', and in turn been badly wounded by defensive fire. Realising that he had to get his aircraft down quickly to stand any chance of survival, Szameitat attempted a forced landing in woods near Buckeburg. He almost pulled it off, but at the last moment the aircraft ground-looped, killing the crew – he was posthumously awarded the *Ritterkruez* in April.

Disaster struck again later that month when on 21/22 January Hauptmann Manfred Meurer, *Kommandeur* of I.Gruppe NJG 1, and a leading ace with 65 kills, became the victim of a collision with a Lancaster raiding Berlin. His He 219A-0 (Wk-Nr 190070/'G9+BB') crashed at speed into the unsuspecting bomber, and both aircraft apparently plunged to earth still locked together.

That same night the *Nachtjagd* lost the first of its princes. Prinz zu Sayn-Wittgenstein had taken off from Deelen in 'borrowed' Ju 88C-6 'R4+XM' (Wk-Nr 750 467 – his personal Ju 88 had been wrecked in a crash following yet another collision the previous night) to attack bombers raiding the city of Magdeburg. He duly shot down four aircraft from a mixed force of Lancasters and Halifaxes and was about to make a second attack on a fifth machine that he had only damaged when the Ju 88C-6 was hit, either by an RAF night fighter or fire from bomber gunners.

After ordering his crew, Feldwebel Friedrich Ostheimer and Unteroffizier Kurt Matzuleit to bale out, the prince attempted an emergency landing at Stendal-Borstel airfield. However, dropping too low during the approach, the Ju 88 touched the ground

Close-up of the nose area of a Bf 110G- 4/R1 that landed at Dübendorf, in Switzerland, on 15 March 1944. Hated by some crews when it first appeared, the FuG 202 *Lichtenstein* radar proved the saviour of the night fighter force, for without it far fewer night bombers could have been brought down. Again this aircraft has the starboard wing underside (including the external fuel tank) painted black as a recognition aid (*Price*)

twice and the undercarriage sheared off with the second impact. The machine crashed heavily to earth and part of it burned, but the pilot's body was found nearby with no sign of wounds resulting from enemy action. The conclusion was that Wittgenstein had been thrown clear of the wreckage but succumbed to injuries sustained in the crash.

So died a pilot unrivalled in his dedication to a deadly trade, one who really should not have been flying that night as by all accounts he was on the point of exhaustion. Holding the rank of Major, Sayn-Wittgenstein had 83 victories at the time of his death.

Oberst Kammhuber's tribute to Sayn-Wittgenstein was effusive;

'The night fighters have lost their best. It seems to be the unalterable will of fate that the very best, Richthofen, Mölders and Wittgenstein, should be killed in the full bloom of their youth. The only comfort is in the knowledge of their heroism and immortality.'

It was the start of a bad year for the Germany, but good fortune continued to smile on other *Experten* such as Hans-Joachim Jabs;

'By January 1944 I had managed 25 more victories, bringing my total to 45. In March I received the Knight's Cross and was appointed Kommodore of NJG 1, where I replaced Werner Streib, who became *Inspektor der Nachtjagd*. On 1 May 1944 I was promoted to Oberstleutnant, but remained with NJG 1 until the end of the war.'

To explore new and revised tactical deployment of night fighters, test weapons and equipment, and place the anti-Mosquito effort under a more centralised command, *Nachtjagdgruppe* 10 had also been formed in January. This unit was issued with examples of all the current frontline types, and became an early recipient of new designs such as the Ta 154 in order to perform operational testing.

As Hans-Joachim Jabs stated in the above quote, Werner Streib's great contribution to the Luftwaffe's night fighter arm was rewarded in March when he was named *Inspektor der Nachtjagd*. The downside of this promotion for the great ace was the he would no longer be able to add to his score of 68 kills (three of which were achieved by day), but he continued to offer sound practical advice and to positively influence new developments intended to increase the force's effectiveness.

Among the changes Streib helped to initiate was a new overall colour scheme for most *Nachtjagd* aircraft. He had flown his first operational sortie in an He 219 painted in a very light – virtually white – finish, and other crews soon came to appreciate the better camouflage that light paint offered over dark shades, which tended to reflect available light.

Accidents continued to claim a significant proportion of night fighter crews, seemingly irrespective of experience, and on 3 March the second of the night fighting princes was lost. Prinz zur Lippe-Weissenfeld's Bf 110G-4 (Wk-Nr 720010) 'C9+CD' clipped the ground and crashed during a flight

A side-on view of the Bf 110G4/R1 of 6./NJG 6 that landed in Switzerland in error on 15 March 1944. This aircraft bore an unusual top surface camouflage scheme reminiscent of day fighter paintwork. As always with Luftwaffe paint finishes, variations were often the rule – but some elements of the *Nachtjagd* never relinquished their links with the *Zerstörergruppen*, and they often operated in dual night/day roles (*Price*)

over the Ardennes, and the prince, who had been part of the *Stabschwarm* of NJG 5 for just a matter of weeks, died with his score on 51.

Behind the scenes the *Natchjagd* maintained its school units for training new crews, but there was increasing pressure for these to become operational. Necessity eventually demanded that NJGs 101 and 102 become partial first line units, a training syllabus being maintained until this was no longer necessary.

In March III./KG 3 was renamed I./NJG 7 and, under standard Luftwaffe policy, experienced crews were then posted to form further operational units. Two months later selected personnel were detached to Brieg to swell the nucleus of a new 4.*Staffel* which had already formed at its operational base at Sonftenberg. The flare-dropping sorties previously made by KG 3 were not entirely forgotten, however, and practical, but non-flying, instruction continued for the time being.

Crews were trained to release flares from a shadowing aircraft over the bombers' target area. These flares burned for five minutes, their purpose being to illuminate enemy aircraft against cloud for destruction by the night fighters. The technique had merit, particularly as overcast thus became an asset rather than a drawback, and the flare-dropping aircraft could also operate as normal night fighters once their initial duty had been carried out.

The spring of 1944 saw a slackening off in Bomber Command area attacks on German cities as the Allies geared up to invade the continent. RAF 'heavies' were increasingly required to pound tactical rather than strategic target,s and the *Nachtjagd* was given a slight respite. Certain crews might have refuted this, as the RAF stepped up Mosquito sorties to prevent any complacency on the part of the Reich's nocturnal defenders. Worse still was the fact that early Mosquito night fighter variants had been refined into the Mk XIX, which carried either British AI Mk VIII or American Mk X radar.

But before Bomber Command began flying invasion support sorties, Harris ordered a raid on Nuremberg on the night of 30/31 March. The culmination of the Battle of Berlin, this was one of the most successful nights of the war for the *Nachtjagd*, which claimed most of the 95 Halifaxes and Lancasters lost on the raid.

In moonlit conditions, German ground control assembled a substantial force at two beacons which, by coincidence, were in the path of the bomber stream. No fewer than 82 aircraft were downed en route to the target, which was largely missed by the majority of the 572 Lancasters and 214 Halifaxes that comprised the Main Force, with nine Mosquitos in support. The balance went down on the return flight and the raid became notorious as one of the RAF's most costly operations.

With the invasion looming, Allied fighter-bombers became an even deadlier menace to the *Nachtjagd* than they had previously been, RAF and USAAF tactical aircraft increasingly having the range to operate all over Germany. Night fighter airfields were attacked as a matter of routine, and individual aircraft were also at extreme risk on non-combat flights – as Oberst Jabs found to his cost;

'My most memorable combat occurred in daylight on 29 April 1944 when I was flying my Bf 110 from St Trond to my own base at

Ex-*Zerstörer* pilot Major Werner Hoffmann saw action with both NJGs 2 and 3 during his time with the *Nachtjagd*. A fair number of night fighter *Experten* achieved scores around the 50 mark, and Hoffmann was no exception, downing exactly a 'half-century' nocturnal kills, plus a solitary day victory (*Toliver*)

Flying a P-47D Thunderbolt south-east of Stettin on 11 April 1944, Capt Raymond Care of the 334th FS/4th FG came upon a Bf 110G-4 night fighter. Opening fire, he soon made sure of its fate, scoring his sixth, and last, kill of the war (*Price*)

Arnhem (Deelen), in Holland. In addition to my crew, I also had a side of bacon on board which I had bought in Belgium.

'Flying in 10/10ths cloud cover, I headed lower just before Arnhem, where the clouds began to break. Soon, I could make out single-engined fighters over the airfield which I mistakenly took for our own. In fact they were eight Spitfires Mk IX (of No 132 Sqn), which were almost twice as fast as my Bf 110. It was too late to try to flee into the clouds since I had been seen, so I prepared to defend myself. Turning to face them as the first Spitfire made its pass, I scored some hits and, as the machine turned for another attack, I hastily landed on the airfield, a fresh attack now bringing cannon fire down on my aircraft. Thankfully, (my crew) escaped before the aircraft was totally destroyed, and with it, my side of bacon.'

There was a happy sequel to this story. Jabs continues;

Down in friendly territory after combat and coded 'G9+AA', this Bf 110G-4 was the mount of Major Jabs of Stab./NJG 1. Although the aircraft and Stab letter have been depicted in green, surviving *Nachtjagd* personnel recall that blacks and greys were far more common for such markings, there being little need for night fighters to exhibit the 'standard' Luftwaffe *Staffel* colours (*Lutz*)

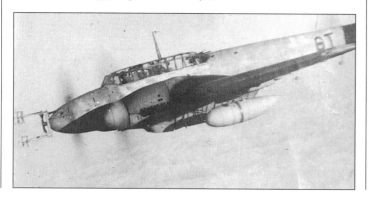

Bf 110G-4 '3C+BT' of 9./NJG 4 based at Juvincourt, in France, was probably photographed on a routine daytime liaison, ferry or courier sortie. Such flights had to be undertaken, but they became increasingly dangerous as Allied fighters ranged further into Germany (*Crow*)

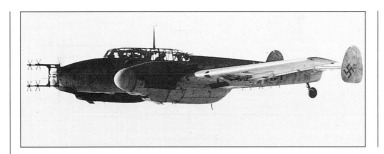

Unusually fitted with ETC bomb racks rather than the more normal drop tanks outboard of the engines, this Bf 110G-4 was probably also part of NJG 4. It was not unusual for night fighters to be called upon to fly other types of war sorties besides night interceptions, but there was always a risk of losing specialist crews to little purpose (*Price*)

'A Spitfire flown by Flt Lt John Caulton had also force-landed, and I learned from him that the attack had been led by Geoffrey Page, the well-known English pilot'.

RAF records confirm that Jabs shot down two Spitfires for his 46th and 47th victories before his Bf 110 was destroyed in the strafing attack – Page was credited with the Bf 110. Years later Jabs met Page at a fighter pilots' convention in Munich. The German fighter ace related the loss of his bacon, and the following Christmas a package of pork arrived at his home with a note from Page saying he was 'frightfully sorry' to have been responsible for the loss of the one in 1944, and hoped that he had now made up for it!

Bf 110G-4 'B4+KA' flown by Feldwebel Kurt Keilig and his crew, Feldwebel Kurt Schroter (radio operator) and Unteroffizier Karl Stamminger (air mechanic). This fighter was one of at least four Bf 110Gs attached to '*Nachtjagd-kommando Norwegen*' in 1945, this small unit otherwise operating Ju 88G-6s. This photo was probably taken at Gardemoen, where Keilig was based prior to being killed trying to rescue German troops trapped by Soviet forces in the Kurland pocket (*Holmes*)

The purposeful lines of the He 219 'Uhu' represented a very advanced design for a specialised night fighter, with a number of novel features including ejector seats, a tricycle landing gear, all-round vision canopy and interchangeable armament combinations. These advantages were offset by crew prejudice against an aircraft that was unable to meet its full potential (*Price*)

Hans-Joachim Jabs (right, with hands on hips) appears to be somewhat displeased with the actions of one of his pilots during a recent sortie. Jabs was an outstanding exponent of the Bf 110, whose score of 50 kills comprised 31 night kills and 19 day victories. The latter total included a couple of Spitfire IXs – not bad for an aircraft encumbered with radar and other weighty equipment (*Jabs*)

The *Nachtjagd*'s area of operations was spread widely, and a presence was more or less maintained in Scandinavia throughout the hostilities. This Ju 88G-6 crew were members of '*Jagdstaffel Norwegen*', their aircraft, coded 'B4+DA' carrying a belly tray with two 20 mm cannon offset to port – there was no built-in nose guns on this version. As this photo was taken in the spring of 1945, they were probably en route to fly a few final sorties over the Kurland pocket which, surrounded by the Red Army, held out until the end of the war. A Ju 88 with this code was downed on a last sortie over Kurland, but the unit clearly remarked another aircraft, as photos exist of it in a derelict state in Germany at a later date (*Maesel*)

That the He 219 was then the only German nightfighter capable of catching a Mosquito was shown on the night of 6/7 May 1944 when Oberleutnant Werner Baake of I./NJG 1 caught one at 26,000 ft. High altitude was not a problem for the German aircrew, for their machine was capable of reaching 41,668 ft. It was the close speed differential that caused most concern. At loaded weight, a Mosquito Mk XIX had a top speed of 378 mph compared to the He 219's speed range of 395 to 466 mph. Mere figures do not indicate the fact that it was unwise for the He 219 crew to run their engines at maximum power for sustained periods of time, and if the lower maximum speed figure is taken as typical (achieved at an altitude of 21,000 ft), it can be seen that the two aircraft were fairly evenly matched.

By the time the Allies invaded continental Europe in June 1944, the *Nachtjagd* had reached its wartime peak of about 800 aircraft (there were 798 aircraft on strength in March according to returns by 8. *Ableitung*). This meant a 35 per cent expansion since 1940, a figure that did not compare too favourably with the virtual doubling of the

German day fighter force in the same time. There would be a gradual reduction in strength from that point until the end of the war.

Thus far, aircraft of the RAF had represented almost the entire enemy force encountered by the *Nachtjagd*, but on 3 July 1944 the first night mission by a Ninth Air Force P-61 Black Widow unit was flown by the 422nd Nightfighter Group from Scorton, England. Large and well-armed, with a top speed of about 370 mph, the P-61B had a normal range of 1400 miles. It would be some time before P-61s encountered manned German aircraft however, for their first months of combat were spent on anti-V1 flying bomb patrols.

In July 4./NJG 3 was formed at Lister, in Norway, an area of operations that the unit, widely known as '*Nachtjagdstaffel Norwegen*', was to remain in for the duration of the war. It moved later in the year to Nautsi, in northern Finland, but returned to Lister in October 1944 before finally transferring to Kjevik in February 1945. The Staffel's Ju 88s were usually scrambled to catch RAF aircraft that had strayed over Scandinavia en route to and from their targets in Germany.

A nightfighter presence in Scandinavia was boosted by short-dura-

'*Jagdstaffen Norwegen*' crews with the ubiquitous 'Staffelhund' cradled in the arms of the man fifth from right. The otherwise plain light grey overall finish of the Ju 88G-6 is relieved by the spiral designs on the propeller spinners for the Jumo engines (*Maesel*)

This Do 217N-2 (Wk-Nr 1570), coded '3C+IP', of 6./NJG 4 was flown into Dübendorf by Feldwebel G Konzac. Well shown are the four-bladed propellers and exhaust flame dampers for the DB 601 engines, plus the FuG 202 radar aerials on the nose and outer wing panels (*Hooks*)

As far as the Luftwaffe was concerned, one of the most costly landings by a Ju 88 during the war took place at Woodbridge, Suffolk, on 13 July 1944. By flying a reciprocal course, its pilot, Obergefreiter John Mäckle from 7./NJG 2, inadvertently gave the RAF the fullest possible data on SN-2, *Flensburg* and *Naxos*, all of which were fitted to the Ju 88G-1 (Wk-Nr 712273/'4R+UR'). This prize did not mean total British radar superiority from then on, but remedial steps saved an untold number of RAF bombers which up until then were literally telling the German night fighters exactly where they were by leaving their radar and IFF transmitters on for most of the time they were over enemy territory (*MAP*)

tion detachments of the regular units based in Germany, including NJG 1 and further elements of NJG 3. A few pilots of the latter's 10.*Staffel* were seconded to Lister during the autumn of 1943 specifically to counter the regular courier flights by the British Overseas Airways Corporation between Scotland and Sweden.

UNUSUAL ADVERSARIES

On the night of 6/7 July NJG 6 scored a succession of relatively easy kills over enemy bombers which the participating crews reported as Wellingtons. Accurate aircraft recognition was understandably difficult in the heat of combat, but these particular victims were so unusual that the briefing officer might have raised an eyebrow even if the German flyers had been spot on. They were B-26 Marauders of the 322nd Bomb Group, flying only their second operational night mission. In a disastrous night the group lost nine aircraft to fighter attack with two others badly damaged (see *Combat Aircraft 2 - Marauder Units of the*

'The British are coming!' Wolfgang Falck at the *Gefechtsstand* at *Luftflotte Reich* HQ in Berlin. Falck is pointing out something of interest to Oberleutnant Wever, son of the famous general who was C-in-C of the pre-war Luftwaffe, and an advocate of long-range bombing before being killed in an air crash at Dresden in 1938 (*Falck*)

Compass alignment and gun harmonisation were just two of the tasks that had to be carried out before frontline aircraft could take off, irrespective of the prevailing conditions. This Ju 88G, fitted with SN-2, makes a draughty perch for the greatcoated men responsible for its servicing (*Price*)

Eighth and Ninth Air Forces for details).

For their part the American crews also mistook the type of aircraft that attacked them. Survivors of the mission reported their attackers as 'Me 410s', which became the favoured nocturnal attackers for units of the Ninth Air Force during their brief spell as tactical night bombers. NJG 6 flew only Bf 110s at that time, and among the successful crews in this particular combat was that of Oberleutnant Schulte (pilot), Herbert Myer (MBF) and Unteroffizier Friedrich Fischer (BS), which scored the first kill at 2210 hrs. The last aircraft fell at 0205 hrs, this aircraft being the second victim of Hauptmann Leopold Fellerer and his crew in III./NJG 6. Two B-26s were destroyed by Oberleutnant Wilhelm Johnen of 8./*Staffel*, and 'doubles' were claimed by Unteroffizier Willi Lauterbach, and Oberleutnants Wolfgang Knieling, Thun and Kraft. A further claim was made by Oberfeldwebel Sawert to bring the total to 14 aircraft, although only nine B-26s were actually lost to fighters by the 322nd. Two Bf 110s were downed, including that of Wolfgang Knieling, who was killed, along with his BS Obergefreiter Helmut Neumann. One Messerschmitt was apparently shot down by flak.

Among the German night fighters that landed in the wrong country for various reasons was this brand new Bf 110G-4/R3 flown by 34-kill ace Oberleutnant Wilhelm Johnen (*Staffelkapitän* of 5./NJG 5), which put down at Dübendorf on 28 April 1944 after having an engine knocked out by Swiss flak whilst chasing an RAF bomber that had strayed into neutral airspace – Johnen had already downed a bomber earlier in the sortie, taking his tally at the time to 18. Incensed at the risk of the aircraft's equipment falling into Allied hands, Göring 'traded' 12 Bf 109G-6s for a guarantee of the Bf 110's destruction, which duly occurred on 19 May 1944 in the presence of German observers – but not before the fighter had been dismantled by Swiss technicians, who fully documented all its electronics! (*Lutz*)

Close up of the tail of Johnen's aircraft in Switzerland, showing 17 of his eventual 34 kills marked on the fin in the 'traditional' manner of the *Nachtjagd* – a white bar with a diagonal red stripe surmounted by a roundel (or other national insignia, as appropriate) and the date of the kill. Johnen described this aircraft with great affection, claiming 'She looked a trifle virginal for she was painted near white from nose to tail; but the cannon muzzles looked far from innocent' (*Lutz*)

Martin Drewes was among the leading night fighter *Experten*, with 49 kills, 43 of which were scored at night (*Toliver*)

By the end of July NJG 1 had taken delivery of a single example of the Ta 154 for further operational testing, and two of the new Ju 88G-6s had been delivered. Production of the latest version of the Ju 88 night fighter rapidly increased so that by 30 September there were 84 in service, compared with 534 Ju 88G-1s available for operations on the same date. In addition the *Nachtjagd* still had 91 Ju 88C-6s and 29 Ju 88R-2s on strength.

For the British flyers one of the worst aspect of bomber operations was often not knowing exactly what had destroyed the aircraft flown by close friends and colleagues. Bombers would simply explode for no apparent reason. It was not until mid-1943 that aircraft returned home with concrete evidence that the Germans had upward-firing cannon in their night fighters. Little could be done to counter this deadly weapon as the Halifax and Lancaster had their H_2S radar scanners fitted aft of the bomb bay, leaving no room for what was really needed – a manned gun turret. *Schräge Musik* remained effective until the end.

The well-established Halifax, Lancaster and Mosquito would equip the frontline squadrons for the rest of the war, although they were not the only RAF aircraft encountered by the Luftwaffe at night. The 'war of the ether' required the services of the B-24 Liberator and B-17 Fortress in Bomber Command's No 100 Group, plus older British types engaged on 'special duty' flights. Unfortunately for the German night fighter crews, the efforts of No 100 Group were almost entirely directed at them. Units within the group were dedicated to destroying enemy aircraft and neutralising equipment that posed a threat to Bomber Command. On most counts, they were highly successful.

The rapid collapse of the Eastern Front during 1944 saw the withdrawal of several Luftwaffe units, among them the original railway nightfighter unit, NJG 100. Stationed near Vienna, the *Geschwader* had a new *Kommandeur* of its II.*Gruppe* from 13 October in the shape of Hauptmann Paul Zorner. One of the leading *Experten* of the *Nachtjagd*, Zorner had flown with his Bordfunker Heinrich Wilke since his days with NJG 2, and the two men had subsequently remained together as a team through transfers to NJGs 3 and 5.

Having participated in 58 of Zorner's kills, it was more than appropriate for Wilke to be decorated with the *Ritterkreuz* (on 6 December 1944), being he was one of the few radio operators rather than pilots to be so honoured. Remaining with NJG 100 until the end of the war, Zorner scored his 59th, and last, night victory in January 1945, by which time he had flown 108 war sorties.

The closing stages of the war in the East saw a motley collection of aircraft types deployed by the Germans at night, the Fw 189A, for example, being pressed into service as a night interceptor with NJG

Interesting close up of a Ju 88, festooned with aerials for both FuG 202 *Lichtenstein BC* and SN-2 radars, undergoing maintenance (*Creek*)

100 and other units. Fitted with FuG 212 radar and a single 20 mm cannon in a *Schräge Musik* installation, this and other types coped with the nocturnal incursions of Soviet aircraft over the German lines.

On the Western front Hitler chose 16 December to counter-attack through the Ardennes under a weather front that grounded Allied tactical air forces. When conditions improved the air action over the 'Bulge' included elements of the *Nachtjagd* tasked with hazardous night ground attacks. These sorties were separate to those of the regular night interceptors, any wastage of experienced crews having to be accepted in an effort to exploit the lower level of Allied tactical air activity during the hours of darkness.

Only limited success was achieved by the *Nachtschlachtgruppen* as the 'Bulge' was duly straightened and the Allied armies rolled on. Over the front the year ended with inevitable additions to the Luftwaffe casualty list. Among those lost was Hauptmann Heinz Strüning, 56-victory *Experte* of NJG 2 who was killed in action on Christmas Eve.

LAST KILLS

As the last year of the war began, the *Nachtjagd* continued as best it could to offer resistance to the RAF bomber offensive, but in sustaining its level of relative ineffectiveness, it had problems, not the least of which was that the well-controlled flak-fighters co-operation of earlier years had all but broken down. With little liaison between the two organisations, the batteries now fired at the discretion of the crews, in any weather, to all heights and as long as was deemed necessary. Although this situation was known to the *Nachtjagd*, it was nonetheless an unwelcome additional hazard to contend with, and friendly aircraft were still mistakenly shot down by flak batteries (as they had been in small numbers throughout the war). Having largely overcome the teething troubles associated with the He 219, I./NJG 1 boasted an inventory of 40 operational aircraft as the new year opened. This *Gruppe* remained the only one to fully re-equip with the Uhu, although examples were delivered to II./NJG 1 and IV./NJG 1, III./NJG 5 and NJGr 10. These units continued to battle Mosquitos when the occasion arose, the RAF having meanwhile upped the stakes by introducing its last wartime nightfighter version, the NF XXX. If anything even more potent than earlier Mosquito marks, the NF XXX commenced operations in late 1944.

Allied fighter-bombers destroyed an untold number of night fighters on the ground throughout Germany, their gun camera film often turning up evidence of new types in service. That was the case with this still, USAAF intelligence, although aware of the existence of the He 219 through examining vertical views of the aircraft taken by PRU aircraft, having seen no obliques of the potent Uhu up to this point. The rather blurred combat photograph therefore caused considerable interest in the wake of its exposure – the machine under fire is probably a He 219A-0 (*Price*)

Attrition continued to take its grim toll of both the inexperienced men of the *Nachtjagd* and its *Experten*. On 8 February the name of 46-kill ace Major Paul Semrau was added to the list of the 'Gefallen' – he was the second most successful *Experte* to begin his career at the controls of a Ju 88C of NJG 2. Semrau was downed in Ju 88G-6 Wk-Nr 620562 by a marauding Spitfire whilst attempting to land at Twente.

Among the *Experten* of the *Nachtjagd* who scored their final victories in 1945 was Hans-Joachim Jabs. On 21/22 February the RAF sent 1110 heavy bombers to Duisberg, Worms and the Mittelland Canal, the latter waterway being the target for 165 Lancasters and 12 Mosquitos. From this force Oberst Jabs shot down two Lancasters for his 49th and 50th kills, thus bringing his total of night victories to 31.

Victories continued to be accrued by Heinz-Wolfgang Schnaufer, however, who had become Kommodore of NJG 4 the previous November. Remaining largely a Bf 110G formation, this unit was thus led by the top-scoring nightfighter pilot of the war, for Schnaufer's tally was never overtaken. Like Jabs, Schnaufer exacted a heavy toll on the Lancasters on 21/22 February, his haul of nine bombers taking his score to 116.

By this time Schnaufer had honed his interception technique to the point of being able to recognise the two main types of RAF heavy bomber simply by the type of exhaust glow they inevitably emitted. As he said at the time;

'When closing in for identification, the first indication would be the silhouette. Then, on the Halifax the exhausts could be seen faintly at 400-500 m (640-800 ft) from below. With the Lancaster, the exhausts could only be seen when the fighter was flying directly astern and in line with it. On a dark night these exhaust patterns would sometimes be visible at a range of 2500 ft (1560 m).'

Commenting generally on how RAF bombers defended themselves against night fighters, Schnaufer stated, 'They do not fire nearly enough rounds, or open fire soon enough, for fear of giving away their position'.

Improved radars were due to come into Luftwaffe service had the war lasted, but the *Nachtjagd* was offered few electronic countermeasures to disrupt the RAF night offensive before hostilities ceased – certainly nothing on the scale that the enemy was regularly bringing to bear over Germany at night. Passive counter-measures were resorted to with some success to cover the *Nachtjagd* under a protective cloak of confusion. They included creating spoof aircraft in the area of the bomber stream by dropping *Duppel* and exchanging large amounts of R/T traffic to give the impression that more night fighters were active than was the case. The latter measures were conducted on both an ad hoc basis and an organised method known as *Orgelpeife* (Pipe Organ). In this, selected crews of single aircraft in one *Staffel* were vectored under 'Y' service control to an area near the estimated target area.

As the raid approached, the voice transmissions would begin. It was important to position the nightfighters realistically close to the stream to engender maximum doubt in the minds of the bomber crews, otherwise the effort would be wasted. *Orgelpeife* aircraft are known to have been part of III./NJG 2 and III./NJG 3, and one operator,

A positive report from a subordinate appears to please the leading *Experte* of the *Nachtjagd*, Major Heinz-Wolfgang Schnaufer (*Toliver*)

Oberfeldwebel Gellner, was able to imitate various German regional dialects so well that his single aircraft was reliably reckoned to appear as 12 to the opposition! Gellner, an actor before the war, could also adopt different vocal tones to heighten the illusion of numbers.

As the war dragged towards its inevitable conclusion, so Bomber Command's list of worthwhile targets dwindled – many major cities had been completely devastated in previous raids, and there was little gain in adding more high explosive to rubble. Raids during this period were therefore targeted against more specific industrial centres, which Lancasters and Halifaxes, invariably with Mosquito support, could now bomb with great precision.

Aside from industrial centres, raids now started to be flown against smaller towns, with devastating effect. These centres were being hit principally because Harris had by then worked far down his list of major target cities. One raid was often all it took to destroy a town. For example, on 3/4 March 1945 the target was principally the synthetic oil plant at Bergkamen, which 234 Lancasters and Halifaxes damaged beyond repair, while a similar sized force of Lancasters wrecked the Ladbergen aqueduct on the Dortmund-Ems Canal. The indomitable Schnaufer notched up two more victories from the aircraft attacking the latter target, seven Lancasters being lost in total.

On 7/8 March the RAF bombed Dessau for the first time, and concurrently sought out oil refinery targets located in Hemmingstedt and Harburg. The Bf 110Gs of NJG 4 were active once again, and the three enemy aircraft that fell to the Kommodore's guns included his 121st, and last, victim of the war. Schnaufer, in common with numerous other *Nachtjagd Experten*, had formed an unbeatable team with his

The real answer to the Germans' long standing problem of finding an effective '*Moskito-Jäger*' was the Me 262. Although this A series prototype (Wk-Nr 170056) carries the aerial array for the *Neptun* radar set, the majority of night kills against Mosquitos and other Allied types are understood to have been made by standard single-seat day fighters vectored onto their targets by GCI

highly skilled crewmen and the venerable Messerschmitt 'twin', which had performed so outstandingly well throughout the force's entire existence. In Schnaufer's case, his impressive score was invaluably assisted by radio operator Fritz Rumpelhardt and gunner Wilhelm Gansler. Not every kill was scored by this trio, there inevitably being crew changes throughout such a lengthy operational career, but Rumpelhardt participated in 100 victories, while Gansler reckoned that his own personal score of 'partial' kills totalled 98 while flying with Schnaufer.

A close up of a Ju 88R-2 reveals its BMW engines and an early style gondola, which was dispensed with on the G-series. The SN-2 radar aerials seen here are as 'clean' as they ever got, with strengthened mounting sections at the base of each 'antler' in this instance (*Creek*)

Rows of tiny aeroplane symbols, complete with the date of each kill, adorned the fin of the last Bf 110G flown by Schnaufer, who was dubbed the 'The Night Ghost of St Trond' by the RAF. The kill markings offered mute testimony to the fact that Schnaufer had just become the most successful nightfighter pilot in the world.

NIGHT JETS

Allied night intruders remained a significant threat to *Nachtjagd* operations, and a practical counter to incursions by Mosquitos and, to a much lesser extent, P-61s, remained a priority with the Luftwaffe high command into 1945. Too few positive encounters with Ninth Air Force Black Widows were reported for the Germans to accurately gauge what threat it posed, but they did believe that the USAAF fighter was, like the Mosquito, too fast to intercept. Precious fuel would be wasted in a pointless 'tailchase' of these Allied marauders, and they were often left alone. Not that the threat they posed was forgotten.

After the specially-prepared Bf 109Gs issued to NJG 11 had signally failed to achieve success as Mosquito hunters, the Ta 154 had failed due to poor manufacturing materials and the He 219 had – through no fault of its own – turned in a patchy record for reliability, the focus changed. Only one German type could match the outstanding British aircraft in terms of sheer performance – the Me 262.

There were precious few serviceable jets – not to mention experienced pilots and safe airfields – available even to undertake interceptions of the perceived 'worst threat' of the USAAF day bombers, but *Kommando Welter* (see *Aircraft of the Aces 17 - German Jet Aces of World War 2* for more details) had nevertheless been formed on 11 November 1944 to operate at night. Declared operational at Magdeburg on 17 December as 10./NJG 11, the unit, led by Oberleutnant Kurt Welter, initially commanded an establishment of 12 Me 262s. *General der Flieger* Josef Kammhuber was placed in command of all jet units, and he brought his considerable expertise in nightfighter techniques to bear.

Welter's *Staffel*, which eventually received about 25 Me 262A-1as

Martin Becker's final tally was 58 night victories, and he became a *Ritterkrauzträger* on 1 April 1944. The award of the Oak Leaves followed on 20 March 1945 (*Toliver*)

Tail of a wrecked Bf 110G-4 showing a tally of 33 victories, all achieved in 1944 by a night fighter pilot whose identity unfortunately remains unknown. The tail section is thought to have been taken from an aircraft found by Allied troops at Neubiberg (*Crow*)

A tail attached to a more complete 'canvas' was – this Bf 110G-4 fin was discovered by pilots of the 365th FG 'Hell Hawks'. A single Soviet machine and nine British aircraft were downed by the pilot of this machine, coded '9W+BO', of 6./NJG 101, which had 'scribble' pattern camouflage over its entire upper surfaces when found at Fritzlar (*Lutz*)

and seven B-1a/U1 sub-types, acquitted itself extremely well – in meeting one of the main threats to the conventional nightfighter force, its 48 claimed night and day victories over Mosquitos represented a major reversal for the RAF. Welter himself had previously test flown a prototype Me 262 fitted with *Neptun* radar, but the majority of his personal night kills (20+) were apparently achieved in standard radarless aircraft. His total wartime haul of 35 Mosquitos, claimed whilst flying firstly '*Wild Sau*' Fw 190s and then Me 262s, represented a record Luftwaffe score.

Other pilots did well too. On the night of 21/22 March Feldwebel Karl-Heinz Becker destroyed a Mosquito intercepted in the area of the German capital. His combat report described the action;

'On 21 March I was ordered to scramble against an incoming Mosquito in the Berlin area. Take-off was at 2103 hours. Over the target (I was) greatly impeded by engine trouble. At 2132 I achieved a good firing position and opened fire from below and to the right at a range of 250-150 m (820-490 ft). I witnessed bits of fuselage and wing (of the enemy aircraft) which immediately resulted in flames. Thereupon I pulled up and away, over the target.

'My port engine was damaged by flying debris from the E/A, thus I could no longer observe it. I landed safely back at home base at 2154 hrs. According to the Egon system my attack took place in grid reference GG5/6.'

Two days later Welter scored his third victory with NJG 10, and the twentieth kill for his unit. Another Mosquito illuminated by searchlights, it broke up in the air under the Me 262's cannon fire before exploding. Welter had attacked from the starboard side, astern of the target from 5-10° below. He used just 30 rounds.

Notwithstanding Welter 'high total, Feldwebel Becker's five victories over Mosquitos (out of a final tally of seven), all achieved in March 1945, placed him in second place in the list of pilots who had destroyed the aircraft in multiple numbers while flying the Me 262.

One of the reasons for NJG 11's success over the Mosquito was that there was no necessity for the Messerschmitt pilots to slow down to match the speed of their quarry – the Mosquito's performance, previously such an advantage, was all but nullified. Me 262 day fighter pilots attacking slow heavy bombers found that they had scant little time to line up the target and fire, for unless their pursuit curve was precisely computed, they would overshoot. When attacking a faster aircraft, this problem was significantly reduced for the jet pilots.

Considering the temperamental nature of the Me 262, the presence of a radar operator significantly eased the jet pilots' workload during night interceptions, and training was initiated for radar observer/navigators. But there was little time for many two-man crews to become

Part of the 'Aladdin's Cave' of German aeronautical and technical progress opened by the Allies was this Bf 110G-4, dispersed in woods to hide it from prying Allied eyes. A standard machine, it shows the offset SN-2 dipoles to advantage (*Lutz*)

proficient in flying the Me 262 – one report states that the programme suffered a setback when a radar-equipped two-seater crashed, killing the observer, who nevertheless had reported strong 'blips' on his *Neptun* scope prior to his demise.

Along with other radars, *Neptun* had been the subject of an extensive programme of development. It culminated in the *Atlas Schwabing* sector-panorama search radar, which introduced colour into the CRT displays, and was tailored towards rapid interpretation of presented data for jet pilots. A yellow screen indicated a target at the same height, green indicated that it was lower and red that it was above the fighter.

As the Allies overran more Reich territory, those units that remained operational were forced into a series of base moves. On 12 April 10./NJG 11 moved to Lübeck, where it remained for just nine days before transferring to a site adjacent to the Autobahn at Reinfeld. Long stretches of pre-war road made ideal makeshift runways, having been largely spared the deluge of Allied bombs that rendered many airfields untenable. On 7 May Welter's unit made a final move to Schleswig-Jagel, but had to leave a Me 262B-1a/U1 behind at Magdeburg, reducing its strength to six aircraft – four Me 262A-1as and two B-1a/Us.

Taking its ratio of kills to operational timeframe into account, 10./NJG 11 had become one of the most successful Me 262 units of them all, its success over the Mosquito proving the superiority of turbojets over the best performance reciprocating engines could offer.

Only one member of the *Nachtjagd* is known to have volunteered to

The mystery of exactly what happened to Schnaufer's last Bf 110G (if indeed it was his aircraft, as several postwar historians have strongly refuted the suggestion that the fighter was ever brought back to England) once it arrived in the UK remains unsolved. Even the exact identity of the famous fighter remains open to conjecture. It was almost certainly not the machine seen here at Knokke-Le Zoute during its ferry flight to England on 23 June 1945, although this fighter (Bf 110G-4/R8 Wk-Nr 180560/ '3C+BA' – Air Ministry Number 15) has often been misidentified as Schnaufer's machine in the past. The other popular candidate was been Bf 110G-5/R1 Wk Nr 420031/'3C+AA' (Air Ministry Number 85) which, like '3C+BA', was captured at Eggebek. It too was ferried back to the UK, arriving at Farnborough on 28 July 1945 – both fighters were subsequently scrapped in 1946-47. *Experte* Wilhelm Johnen made the following comment concerning Schnaufer and his final Bf 110 postwar;

'At the end of the war the British transported Schnaufer's crack machine to England. The Londoners were able to admire the Me 110 in Hyde Park. Shaking their heads, they counted the bars representing kills on the tail unit. 124 . . . 126 . . . They would have liked to bring the "Spook of St Trond" to London, but Schnaufer lay in hospital and had no wish to be stared at by the Londoners in Hyde Park'

transfer to Adolf Galland's Me 262-equipped *Jagdverband* 44, this being Major Willi Herget. Having accumulated a day and night victory tally of 73, Herget was the fourth highest-ranking *Experte* in the *Nachtjagd*. He had flown with NJG 3 since 1941, became *Gruppenkommandeur* of I./NJG 4 in late 1942, and subsequently receiving the *Ritterkreuz* from *General der Flieger* Kammhuber in June 1943 when he scored his 30th victory – the Oak Leaves to mark his 63rd victory followed in April 1944.

On 2 January 1945 a staff appointment indirectly saw Herget's involvement in the Me 262 programme, and ultimately led to him seeing action in the type with JV 44. He briefly flew the Me 262A-1a/U4 fitted with a 50 mm MK 214A Mauser cannon in action during his time with Galland's unit.

The Allies found a number of Me 262B-1a/U1 nightfighters – some of them radar-equipped – completely intact on their last operational airfields when hostilities ceased. Numerous examples of other *Nachtjagd* stalwarts were also discovered, and at those locations where German personnel had failed to destroy these operational aircraft, Allied inspection teams were free to test complete working examples of the electronic equipment they had been combating for some two years.

Most of what they found was familiar in respect to capability, but there were pointers as to how future nightfighter operations might have been conducted, as exemplified by the Me 262 – jet day fighters were new enough outside Germany, let alone night interceptors! Just how far German research into advanced aeronautics had progressed

Left
Fitted with SN-2 and FuG 212 aerials on the centreline, the Bf 110 was almost as numerous on the last day of the war as it was on the first – but a few significant changes had been made to the last wartime versions. Among them was the replacement of the 'double pipe' exhaust flame damper with a straight pipe (*Price*)

Found on a wooded dispersal at Lechfeld, Ta 154 Moskito Wk-Nr 320003 had previously been painted in a tactical camouflage scheme. A handful of these aircraft, without radar, were flown operationally by NJG 2 (*Crow*)

Another Ta 154 in a sorry state on the edge of Lechfeld at the time of the German surrender. One of a number of attempts to provide the *Natchjagd* with a more modern aircraft than the Bf 110 and Ju 88, the Moskito failed to realise its potential primarily because of a shortage of reliable adhesives for the wood-bonding of the airframe (*Crow*)

was clear enough, and but for a muddled production programme, political interference, Allied bombing and, most of all, too much dilution of dwindling industrial resources on far too many projects, the Luftwaffe might have been in a position to pose a greater threat to the Allies than it actually was. Every member of the Allied inspection teams became acutely aware of that fact as the extent of the German aeronautical 'Aladdin's Cave' was revealed.

Interrogated by the Allies after the war, Kammhuber swore that with 18 *Nachtgeschwaderen* instead of the six comprised the backbone of his force, he would have been able to achieve that much more, and probably even forced the British to curtail, or change, their heavy bombing policy. Other leading members of the nightfighter force also fell into Allied hands – 'Wolf' Falck was captured by the US 20th Division, while Schnaufer was informally interviewed by an RAF team at Grove, in Denmark, after members of NJG 4 had complied with orders to render their Bf 110Gs unfit to fly by removing the rudders and airscrews. Sadly, the leading *Experte* of the *Nachtjagd* was killed in a car crash in France in July 1950 – a similar fate as to that which befell other pilots in the early postwar years.

More fortunate in that he survived to spend five years in a Soviet prison was Paul Zorner. Having surrendered to American forces near Kalsbad, in Czechoslovakia, on 10 May 1945, he was duly turned over to Soviet troops and not released until January 1950.

Among the many pilots of the *Nachtjagd* who ran up multiple victories, other high scorers included Werner Hoffman of NJGs 3 and 5 with 51, Rudolf Frank of NJG 3 with 45, Josef Kraft of NJGs 1, 4, 5 and 6 with 56, Herbert Lutje of NJGs 1 and 6 with 50 and Heinz Vinke with 54.

'Ribbed' base sections are in evidence in this close up view of the anchorage posts for the SN-2 aerials of a Ju 88G-6 captured by US forces (*Crow*)

Apart from the aircraft that *Nachjagd* painters had had time to mark up with unit identity, US troops found hundreds of new aircraft, fresh from their delivery flights. These 'clean' Ju 88G-6s greeted men of the 6th Armored Division as they investigated Langensalza on 7 April 1945. The machine on the left had its Werk-Nummer stencilled on the undercarriage leg (*Crow*)

At the Luther factory, near Brunswick, despite their dire situation the Germans managed to introduce what amounted to revised camouflage and markings for night fighters, as this Bf 110G-4, and other examples, show. The main difference was that the *Balkenkrauz* markings, previously applied in white, were changed to black, whilst the fuselage and wing top surfaces had a much more defined grey tone in contrast to the well-established light mottle fuselage finish. A yellow rear fuselage band was also used with this scheme (*Crow*)

Many Luftwaffe aircraft were ferried to England for evaluation, including this Ju 88G-6, complete with flame-damping exhausts, a *Naxos* installation and twin 20 mm cannon belly pack (*Price*)

Valuable data, as well as hardware, was gathered from in-depth interrogation of leading *Nachtjagd* officers, including Kammhuber, Martini and Schmid, all of whom prepared full reports, which were closely studied and put to some practical use primarily by the Americans. But neither the Allies – or their erstwhile foe – realised that there would never again be a nightfighter war quite like the one that had just ended in such a hard-won victory at an appalling cost.

As far as the aircraft used by the *Nachtjagd* were concerned, the core types had performed extremely well. Both the Ju 88 and Bf 110 had been adaptations of designs originally intended for other roles, and of these, Messerschmitt's *Zerstörer* more than lived up to its name during the hours of darkness. Discredited ever since in the 'popular press' following its poor showing in the Battle of Britain, the Bf 110 avenged any humiliation it suffered over the Channel in 1940 many-fold as it went on to become, in terms of aerial kills, the most successful nightfighter of all time – and most of its victims were British.

The Ju 88 matured into an outstanding nightfighter, with an excellent range and adequate space to accommodate the extra equipment necessary for the role. Well armed, it too was flown with elan by many of the top nightfighter teams.

A mountain of statistics had been compiled by both sides to show the scale of the war effort, and in the case of the *Nachtjagd*, approximately 7400 enemy aircraft were claimed destroyed – the vast majority of them over the Reich and Western Europe – by the six main *Geschwader* and smaller formations including '*Wilde Sau*' units. This total figure for all war theatres included both night and day victories and, unsurprisingly, showed NJG 1 as the leading unit with 2311 victories. This effort cost the *Geschwader* 135 officers and 541 men killed during the period 26 July 1940 to 8 May 1945.

Some Allied losses can be shown for comparison purposes: total losses of Mosquito nightfighters was 84 aircraft to all causes, including 25 NF XXXs, the majority of which fell to He 219s and Me 262s. These figures compared with 568 examples of all Mosquito marks that 'failed to return' from wartime operations. Against this, Mosquito crews were credited with 249 aircraft shot down, the majority of them night fighters – this total includes 83 Bf 110s by bomber support squadrons in No 100 Group and ten Bf 110s by non-No 100 Group units.

The two squadrons of P-61 Black Widows operational with the Ninth Air Force in Europe (the 422nd and 425th NFSs) claimed respectively 43 and 10 aircraft destroyed, plus a combined total of 7 probables and 7 damaged. Four other USAAF nightfighter units, operating mainly Beaufighters and Mosquitos, probably claimed a small number of nightfighters too.

Terrible though the *Nachtjagd*'s losses were, they were proportionally less, in cold statistical terms, than the sacrifice asked of other Luftwaffe branches – the *Jagdwaffe* for one – to simply lose a war. This naturally reflected the relatively small size of the force throughout hostilities, but *Nachtjagd* survivors, even in defeat, could take justifiable pride in having been part of a technically advanced organisation – one that the enemy had to reckon with until the very end.

Incidentally, the *Nachtjagd*'s history is perpetuated in today's Luftwaffe by 1./JBG 74 'Mölders'. The *Staffel* has taken over the wartime badge, and as 'Wolf' Falck says, 'The pilots now call themselves the "Falken-*Staffel*" – they are the young Falken and I'm the old Falke'.

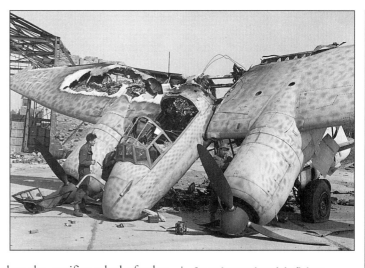

Some interesting night fighter camouflage schemes were revealed in both snapshots taken by troops as they posed with the discarded equipment, and official photos. An example of the latter was this burnt out and radarless Ju 88G, seen on a rubble-strewn ramp at an 'airfield near Brunswick', as the USAAF caption explained

The Imperial War Museum in Lambeth, south London, is today the home of the port fin of the last Bf 110G flown by Heinz-Wolfgang Schnaufer. It had been meticulously decorated by the NJG 4 groundcrew who looked after the aircraft flown by the *Nachtjagd*'s leading *Experte* with 121 victories (*IWM*)

A display at Farnborough in October/November 1945 brought many of the last German combat aircraft to the attention of the press and public. The exhibits included this He 219, complete with SN-2 radar

FIGHTER'S NIGHT

The text in this chapter is drawn almost entirely from wartime interrogation reports covering typical night activity in Luftwaffe units of the *Nachtjagd*. Some additional material has been included for the reader's interest and information.

Each morning after operations, the aircraft were checked over and rearmed. Between 1700 and 2100 hours at the evening briefing, the *Gruppe* was given a meteorological report for the area that it was to cover, and if the weather was favourable to bomber attacks, the unit had to notify its available operational strength to the fighter control centre before dusk. The *Gruppe* was provided with information as to the runway to be used, the chosen orbiting point and alternative aerodromes, whilst a W/T briefing was also given by the signals officer.

In the *Himmelbett* zone of operations, two aircraft were sometimes sent up into each box during the afternoon to carry out vectoring and interception practice for the purpose of helping train ground and air personnel, whilst at the same time making a final check on equipment.

Aircraft to be used for the forthcoming night's operations were lined up before dusk at each side of the runway after having been re-serviced by the ground staff. At Grove, for example, there were usually ten machines parked on the apron at the end of the runway, spaced at intervals of 180 ft. In case of enemy intrusion, these undispersed aircraft would take off so as not to present easy targets.

The balance of the unit's aircraft, including those making up the second alert, were dispersed on, or near, the airfield, camouflaged where

Daylight gaggle of Bf 110Gs of an unidentified unit surrounded by an angry sky. As German fortunes waned, the *Nachtjagd* was sometimes obliged to seek out targets in daylight – a costly and counter-productive business. However, by managing largely to confine their sorties to night interceptions, the force remained potent until the end (*Price*)

possible with tree branches and netting. Care was taken to wipe out all traces of taxy tracks from dispersal points to the aerodrome.

When operating under *Himmelbett* control, two aircraft of each operational *Staffel* were placed at immediate readiness of five minutes. If one aircraft was scrambled, the second was to stand by to take the place of the first if the latter should encounter any last minute trouble such as engine failure. The crew of the second fighter remained in their aircraft for possible immediate take-off until the airborne fighter was known to have reached its assigned box, after which the second crew could return to the dispersal, but were to remain alert for a further call.

Under the '*Wilde Sau*' system, the single-engined fighters of an entire *Staffel* or a particular *Gruppe* were readied. Typically, the first *Staffel* was at immediate readiness, with the third at 15 minutes' stand by. This procedure varied according to the tactical disposition: on '*Wilde Sau*' operations I./JG 301, when charged with defending its allocated area of northern France, divided into two sections. The first comprised 60 per cent of *Gruppe* strength and the second 40 per cent.

When Allied aircraft were expected over northern France the first section would take off within 15 minutes and be followed, if necessary, by the remainder. However, in protracted operations the second section would take off two hours after the first, by which time the first aircraft would be returning to refuel.

In general '*Wilde Sau*' pilots were divided into three 'weather grades': (a) those with most experience, who were expected to fly in any weather; (b) those with limited experience, only ordered up in certain conditions; and (c) newcomers who would fly in only the best conditions. Pursuit night fighting, particularly when the RAF night offensive was at its peak, often demanded that the entire *Staffel*, or even *Gruppe*, was kept available for immediate use. Major Ruppel, air operations officer for the middle Rhine area, divided his pilots into two categories – those who could get off the ground in three minutes, and those who took five minutes.

NJG 6, based in southern Germany, had four readiness states:

(1) - 80 minutes: operations not expected. Crews were allowed to remain in their quarters and sleep.

(2) - 30 minutes: crews were to stay in their quarters, but dressed and ready for flight, with the possibility of take-off within 30 minutes.

(3) - 15 minutes: crews were to be in the 'ready room' near their allocated aircraft's hardstands, ready for flight.

(4) - immediate: crews were to sit in their aircraft, to be ready for take-off within two minutes.

Any changes or updates in the prevailing situation were relayed to the crews by loudspeakers in the dispersals and hangars. Very signals from the control tower told pilots to start their engines and taxy to the end of the runway. Actual take-off was usually ordered over the R/T for the twin-engined fighters operating under the *Himmelbett* or *Pursuit* systems, while '*Wilde Sau*' aircraft usually took off on Very light signal.

A one-minute interval was allowed for each twin-engined aircraft to take-off, 30 seconds for single-seaters. It was therefore possible to have, if necessary, the entire nightfighter force airborne within 30 minutes.

Tranquil scene at a *Nachtjagd* base, with a newly-delivered replacement Bf 110G being serviced prior to the application of unit codes (*Lutz*)

In NJGs 2 and 6, an entire *Gruppe* would be airborne in 20-24 minutes, with the first one getting all its aircraft away within eight minutes of the initial warning being received.

In the event of double sorties being flown by individual crews, those who returned to their base airfield would resume the original state of readiness. Should they have cause to divert to an alternate airfield, they would be temporarily attached to the unit they had 'visited', and be briefed as though they belonged to that unit.

Under the *Himmelbett* system, the night fighter would normally patrol the searchlight belt to which it had been assigned – it would fly continually between two given points at altitudes between 12,000 and 18,000 ft. In areas were RAF bombers were expected to be encountered, standing patrols would be maintained in the *Himmelbett* boxes from dusk onwards. Duration of patrols depended on the aircraft type, Ju 88s and Do 217s typically remaining airborne for three hours and the Bf 110 for two. Patrols would be flown at altitudes roughly similar to those adopted by the enemy bomber stream, both to avoid any conflict with the smooth operation of local flying in training areas at lower altitudes, and to evade intruders.

When the *Himmelbett* system was changed, standing patrols were largely abandoned, these being further curtailed as petrol shortages took effect. Fighters were generally scrambled on warnings received, but as the Luftwaffe lost its early warning coverage as the Allies captured more territory, the retreat into Germany reduced the standing patrol until it was a thing of the past. An additional hazard at that time were enemy intruders. This was where the pursuit system came into its own, as aircraft would take-off and make for a particular beacon shortly before receiving orders to proceed to the operational area.

The risk of collision was reduced by all aircraft making a left hand orbit of the beacon at different altitudes – stepped up to 9800 ft (3000 m), with each crew maintaining 100 m (160 ft) separation – which meant that as many as 30 machines could be in a small area at one time without running the risk of collision. The *Gruppe* commentary would then pass a bearing for interception. Searchlights continued to play their part in night interceptions throughout the war, and under the pursuit system, they were sometimes used as controlling aids in locating the bomber stream – lights would be dipped to point the fighters in the right direction.

Following standard operating procedure, interception tactics depended on the type, and capability, of the equipment used, and weather conditions, particularly the extent and altitude of any cloud.

The fundamental aspects of target approach using *Lichtenstein BC*, FuG 218 and FuG 220 saw the attacker come in from directly behind and slightly below the bomber at a controlled speed, closely co-ordinated with that of the 'bogey'. The logical exception would be in the event of an illuminated layer of cloud forming a background below, in which case the fighter approached from above to avoid detection by his own silhouette. Speed control was important, both for recognition purposes and to allow the pilot to set up an attack of his own choosing.

During a target approach using radar, the fighter had to modify its speed to the decreasing distance between the two aircraft so that at the moment of visual pick up (depending on the prevailing visibility), both were flying at approximately the same speed.

In most cases of approach using AI equipment, it was the responsibility of the Bordfunker to pass the necessary changes of direction to the pilot. One exception to this general rule occurred when the FuG 240 *Berlin* equipment was used. In that case the Bordfunker merely had to centre the target on his CRT and the target direction would register on an indicator in the pilot's cockpit. Thus, the pilot himself analysed the target's relative position, and manoeuvred his aircraft accordingly.

The time at which the Bordfunker would turn on his equipment was entirely dictated by circumstances. As one operator stated;

'The SN-2 was switched on for short periods when the operator, either from data from the ground or visual observation of flares, believed that he was near the bomber stream. There were no orders governing the length of time it was to be switched on. It was general policy, nevertheless, to turn on the low tension (circuit-heating) when the night fighter received its original vector from ground control – not before.'

Ground control aimed to place the fighter immediately behind the enemy aircraft, but the pilot could request that he be positioned to port or starboard, dependent on the available light conditions and the source of such light. Night fighters were normally vectored to the same height as the hostile aircraft or, by request, to heights decreasing to 490 ft (150 m) below it.

When the night fighter was within about 6500 ft (4062.50 m) of the target, the transformer (high tension) of the *Lichtenstein* was switched on. In some cases it was switched on at up to 9800 ft (6125 m) away, but only an exceptional operator could obtain satisfactory contact at more than 6500 ft distance.

As soon as contact had been established the Bordfunker gave the codeword 'Emil-Emil' ('I have made contact'). The code for being within visual and firing range was 'Ich Beruhre'. Ground control could always be called back in case the target was lost through taking evasive action. It usually took between six to ten minutes to secure a contact after receiving the first vector from ground control. On occasion, a fighter with a radar, or good visual contact, would be instructed to chase the enemy aircraft beyond GCI range – for example, fighters based in Holland sometimes fol-

Despite the 'eleventh hour' having tolled for Germany, company paint shop workers rarely let new aircraft leave the factories without regulation camouflage and markings, despite the time it took to finish aircraft as large as the Ju 88G. Many night fighters were found in 'as new' condition at Langensalza and other airfields by Allied troops (*Crow*)

lowed RAF bombers as far north-west as the English coast.

The *Naxos* homer, which was standard in the Ju 88, and fitted to many night fighters in conjunction with SN-2, led to the adoption of an original night interception technique. Limited in that it could be used effectively only against aircraft transmitting radar or navigational data, *Naxos* was widely used and proved very successful. It was able to detect H_2S transmissions as far away as 60 miles, and this capability all but precluded the participation of GCI in the aerial kill. The British radar set was highly directional and created a 'cone' of detectable energy below the transmitting bomber, and German night fighters strove to keep within this area, but low enough to maintain CRT contact.

To find a suitable target the German pilot received a *Naxos* blip, checked the bearing and aligned his course. He then nosed upwards to pull clear of the H_2S cone. The night fighter levelled out when the blip disappeared from the *Naxos* scope, and the pilot would climb in a series of 'steps' to check his position relative to the H_2S cone. By repeating this procedure the fighter avoided detection by any IFF device carried by the bomber.

Naxos was not intended for final approach purposes, but rather to bring the German fighter within range of its SN-2 – although there were some pilots who used the device right into the final phases of interception. At that point the night fighter would open fire without question if the target was identified as a four-engined bomber. The problem came if a twin-engined type was in the sights. In that case the target's identity had to be established before attacking, and in the event that there was insufficient light from flares or searchlights, the quarry had to be followed until its behaviour gave away its nationality.

This sounds vague but it often worked, for there were few Allied pilots who did not adopt some form of evasive action if they were being followed. However, if a twin-engined type could not be visually identified, and it took no evasive action, there was little more that the German crew could do. Exhaust patterns were not much help, as all operational 'twins' on both sides had some form of flame-damping, but under such circumstances both the Mosquito and Black Widow tended to give away their identities by their respective speeds – although a degree of doubt would still remain as the Me 410 also had a high top speed. A German aircraft would, however, be expected to fire a Very light signal if it was being followed.

In the final analysis, a *Nachtjagd* crew was wiser to break off the pursuit if any doubt still remained. There were cases of pilots being court-martialled for shooting down friendly aircraft through failing to make visual confirmation.

On clear nights contrails assisted the night fighter crews, these being useful in estimating the approximate distance of the bombers ahead by the density of the trails. Having flown to the end of the contrail, the fighter would weave from side to side to pick up individual aircraft, for it was almost impossible to see the actual bomber creating a trail.

'*Wilde Sau*' operations brought their own recognition problem in an arena where single-seat fighters had not generally operated. In their early operations, '*Wilde Sau*' pilots would briefly flash their navigation lights seconds before delivering an attack to warn other night fighters of their presence. When the RAF began using Mosquitos over Germany, this practice was forbidden as being too dangerous.

Technically, the German were hampered by not developing a reliable form of IFF (Identification: Friend or Foe). Other than the standard airborne responder IFF set, the FuG 25a, which was installed in most operational aircraft from 1942 onwards and was used by ground stations for recognition purposes throughout the war. The FuG 25a worked well enough in conjunction with *Freya* ground stations and *Egon* control, but it could not operate with the *Wurzburg* ground set without a supplementary attachment in the form of an interrogator.

A secondary method of identification from the ground did exist. This was a system whereby a red light flashed on the control panel of the night fighter when in the beam of a *Wurzburg*. The pilot would depress a switch upon instructions from the ground and reply simply 'yes' or 'no' according to whether or not the light flashed to indicate his position within the beam. If ground control was uncertain as to the identity of the fighter, the latter would be asked to make alternate left or right turns to cause a blip on the *Wurzburg* presentation screen.

Intruding Allied night fighters adversely effected the tactical use of IFF, just as they did most other phases of Luftwaffe night fighting procedure. For some time there was a popular belief that the enemy was able to home onto FuG 25a transmissions, despite being officially told that this was not the case, and that the equipment should be left on at all times during operational flights. Circumventing their orders, many crews still switched off their FuG 25a for fear that they would otherwise be detected. In fact crews were generally wary of any IFF device – they lost faith in such equipment after being continually fired upon by their own flak with the FuG 25a switched on or off! It became standard procedure – if no intruders were reported – to switch on FuG 25a at the point of take-off, and to keep it operating until well clear of the airfield. During intercepts the instrument would be turned off, but on return to base, again providing that no warning of intruders was in effect, the set would be switched on shortly before reaching the airfield.

The fact that British aircraft usually left their IFF sets turned on was a mystery to German crews insomuch as it allowed their own early warning and airborne radars to trip the enemy transmissions for homing and warning purposes. Alternatively, much faith was placed in tail warning equipment – it was known that many crews, contrary to orders, hugged the ground while orbiting a beacon in order to avoid Allied intruders, corkscrewed throughout the course of an interception and, in some cases – particularly with the Ju 88 – carried an extra crewman whose job it was to keep rearward observation, and act as a gunner. Knowing they had a tail warning device relieved tension among crews, and it was generally felt that such protection was both necessary and effective for the prosecution of night fighter tactics.

Tail warning was not infallible, and most crews accepted that a percentage of incomplete interceptions would occur through false warnings being received. All involved agreed, however, that the safety factor more than compensated for this drawback, and that only a small proportion of contacts were lost to this cause. Much depended on the type of tail warning fitted – most sets designed for that purpose merely indicated a target to the rear and gave the range only. In this case the over-taking speed of the pursuing aircraft was taken into account as an aid to determining the character of the pursuit – whether accidental or deliberate. If a moderate but definite rate of closure was noticed, the German fighter would take violent evasive action when the would-be attacker reached a position within 1500 ft, although sometimes the critical closing range was allowed to reduce to much less than 1300 ft, this factor depending upon the individual crew's nerves!

Evasive action in such an instance was recommended as a 180° hard turn to port or starboard. It the pursuing aircraft could be seen by the crew, the turn would be made in accordance with its position. In the days when enemy intruders were still relatively rare in German skies the night fighters were briefed to peel off towards an aircraft following them, but this manoeuvre resulted in a loss of 5000 to 6500 ft in height, which took about ten minutes to regain.

Naxos could also indicate (in azimuth only) the presence of an Allied fighter using its 10-centimetre SCR 720 radar, and it had the advantage of picking up such a signal from as far away as 50 miles – providing that the enemy aircraft was somewhat above. *Naxos* could therefore act as a tail warning aid by supplementing the much shorter range of the radar's purpose-built for tail warning.

EVE OF DESTRUCTION

Once enemy aircraft had been identified as hostile there were several standard procedures designed to destroy them, and their use depended on prevailing orders and individual crew experience. In some units the tactics preferred by the commanding officer would be followed by the crews under his command. The actual method of approach was usually left to each crew, night fighting having always been more of a 'lone wolf' method of attack than other forms of aerial warfare, dictated both by the situation they found themselves in and the type of armament fitted to their aircraft.

With normal fixed forward-firing guns, attacks were nearly always from astern and below, owing to the fact that most German night fighter types had bad downward visibility. British bombers were generally poorly defended from below, and they were usually seen more clearly when silhouetted against the sky.

The usual attack was proceeded by throttling back at the limit of visual range. Then, after deciding on his particular type of pass, the pilot would open up to full throttle and close to firing range. A type of attack favoured by IV./NJG 1 was for the fighter to make a slow approach until it was about 150 ft immediately beneath the target bomber, and then fly along at a synchronised speed until the pilot was ready to fire. It was claimed that in this position, the fighter could not be seen by the bomber's crew and was not covered by any of its guns. The actual attack was made by pulling up almost vertically and sending a burst of fire along the underside of the bomber's wings. Although this method was very popular in IV./NJG 1, it was apparently regarded as dangerous by other units, who stressed the danger element of the bomber diving or releasing its load just as the night fighter was about to fire

Two other methods were; (1) the pilot aimed ahead of the bomber and fired as he pulled up from below so that the bomber flew into the stream of shells which sprayed along the length of the fuselage; and (2) a tactic generally confined to the lighter Bf 110 was to pull up perpen-dicularly and turn away in either direction while delivering a burst which raked the bomber's wings from tip to tip.

With *Schräge Musik* installations the approach was identical, but slightly lower. This armament was not universally popular, particularly with older pilots who preferred to use the fixed forward-firing guns they had trained with and become accustomed to. It was the younger crews who favoured the newer upward firing guns, as some of them tended to open fire with conventional weapons from beyond maximum range, thus giving their position away, and allowing the target to take evasive action. One disadvantage with *Schräge Musik* was that if the target bomber exploded, the night fighter was in danger of being right in the path of burning debris.

On the other hand, it was extremely difficult to stay below a bomber that was taking diving evasive action. The new armament rapidly gained in favour despite the prejudice of the old hands, and Schnaufer for one estimated that in the latter stages of the war, 50 per

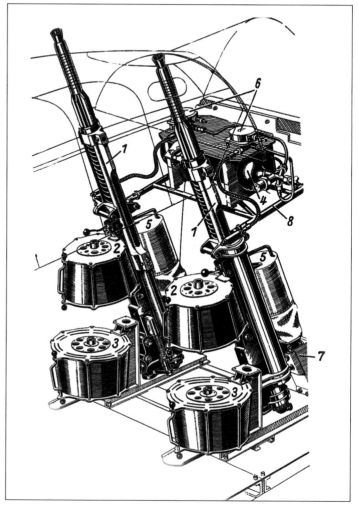

Above and left
Managing to become something of a Luftwaffe secret weapon, the *Schräge Musik*-type installation was almost as old as air warfare itself, had anyone cared to check the records. The RAF, to its cost, neglected to do so, and the type of installation seen here proved deadly when it was fired upwards into the unprotected bellies of RAF bombers. All British types were vulnerable to attack from this quarter (*Price*)

Complete with a twin-cannon *Schräge Musik* installation, this Ju 88G-6 has the mounting for a tail-warning radar below the rudder – a standard fitting of many of the G-series

Neubiberg was full of surprises in the summer of 1945. Its resident aircraft included this heavily-dappled, and SN-2-equipped, Ju 88G-1 ('U5+IT') of 9./KG 2, sharing the dispersal area with other dedicated Ju 88 night fighters. Machines of this unit probably operated as night pathfinders, dropping flares to illuminate enemy bombers for destruction by standard night fighters (*Crow*)

cent of night fighter attacks were carried out with upward-firing guns. '*Wilde Sau*' attacks were commonly delivered in a steep climb after a dive from a height of 1300 ft (400 m) above the bomber.

At night fighter schools pilots were taught to aim at the undersides of the bomber, between the engines and wing roots, in the hope of setting the fuel tanks on fire, and a number of *Experten* were indeed skilled enough to be this exacting. In actual combat the less experienced crews foreswore trying to hit vulnerable spots, as they often found it hard enough to hit the enemy aircraft at all.

Average range for opening fire was about 400 ft, although the more experienced pilots would narrow the gap down to around 200 ft. Breakaway, once a kill was certain, was in a diving turn to avoid any falling debris.

Crews showed a marked preference for attacking four-engined aircraft. For one thing, they were (compared to 'twins' such as the Wellington) faster, and therefore easier for the night fighter to synchronise speeds. When intercepting a Lancaster or Halifax, there was rarely any necessity for the fighter to lower the flaps in order to avoid overshooting.

For their part, the RAF bomber crews employed passive defence against German fighters, using the highly effective corkscrew and, to a lesser extent, weaving. The latter tactic was reported as early as 1943 not to have been so effective, as bomber crews generally followed too shallow a flight path (probably for fear of collision) while it was being executed. Sideslipping in a semi-stall and losing height rapidly could also shake off a night fighter.

Nachtjagd crews reported that bombers returning from the Ruhr adopted another tactic that could frustrate them. After clearing the target area, the bombers tended to reduce height steadily until reaching the Dutch coast at about 300 ft. This caused them not only to pass through the night fighter control areas at the greatest possible speed, but also to be low enough to render attacks from below difficult.

When the bombers opened fire on attacking night fighters, the use of tracer rounds had a definite deterrent effect on the majority of German crews, as did the rarely-used ploy of exploding a flash bomb to the rear of the bomber under attack. Both kinds of reaction temporarily blinded the night fighter pilot long enough for him to lose sight of the target, and in many cases for the bomber to escape.

APPENDICES

Leading *Experten* of the *Nachtjagd*

Name	Final score	*Nachtjagd* Unit(s)		
Schnaufer, Heinz-Wolfgang	121	NJGs 1 and 4		
Lent, Helmut	102 (113)	NJGs 1, 2 and 3		Died 7/10/44 after accident on 5/10/44
zu Sayn-Wittgenstein, Prinz Heinrich	83	NJGs 2, 3 and 5	KIA 21/1/44	
Meurer, Manfed	65	NJGs, 1 and 5		
Radusch, Günther	65	NJGs 1, 2, 3 and 5		
Streib, Werner	65 (68)	NJG 2	KIA 21/1/44	
Rökker, Heinz	64	NJG 2		
Schoenert, Rudolf	64 (65)	NJGs 1, 2, 5 and 100		
Zorner, Paul	59	NJGs 2, 3, 5 and 100		
Raht, Gerhard	58	NJGs 2 and 3		
Becker, Martin	58	NJGs 3, 4 and 6		
Herget, Wilhelm	57 (73)	NJGs 3 and 4		
Francsi, Gustav	56	NJG 100		
Kraft, Josef	56	NJGs 1, 4, 5 and 6		
Strüning, Heinz	56	NJGs 1 and 2	KIA 21/12/44	
Welter, Kurt	56 (63)	JG 300 and NJG 11		
Frank, Hans-Dieter	55	NJG 1	KIFA 27/9/43	
Vinke, Heinz	54	NJG 1	MIA 26/2/44	
Geiger, August	53	NJG 1	KIA 29/9/43	
Hoffmann, Werner	51 (52)	NJGs 3 and 5		
zu Lippe-Weissenfeld, Prinz Egmont	51	NJGs 1 and 5		
Greiner, Hermann	50 (51)	NJG 1		
Lütje, Herbert	50	NJGs 1 and 6		
Drewes, Martin	49	NJG 1		
Kollak, Reinhard	49	NJGs 1 and 4		

() = Final score, including day fighter claims

KIA = Killed in action

KIFA = Killed in flying accident

MIA = Missing in action

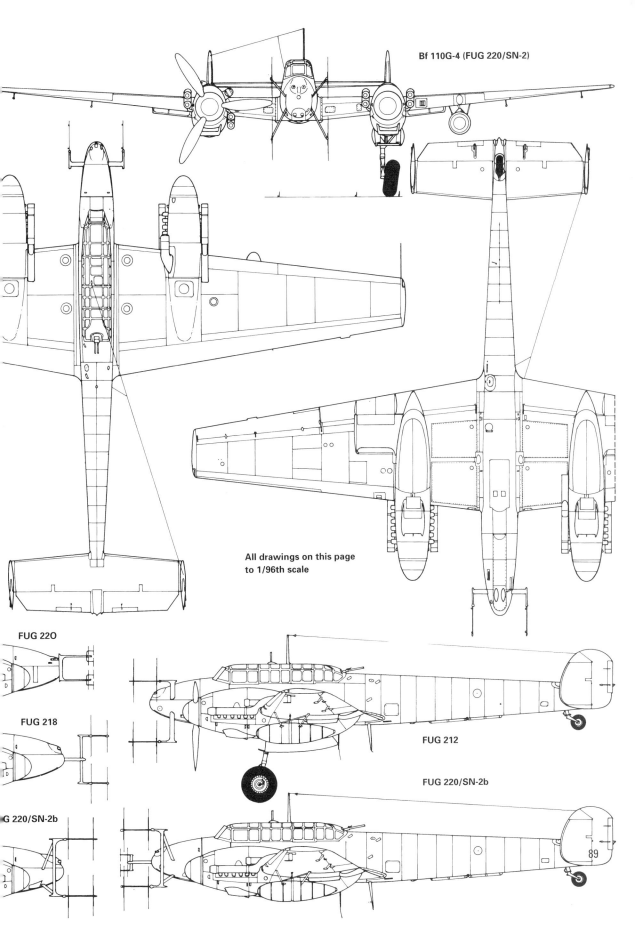

Bf 110G-4 (FUG 220/SN-2)

All drawings on this page
to 1/96th scale

FUG 22O

FUG 218

G 220/SN-2b

FUG 212

FUG 220/SN-2b

89

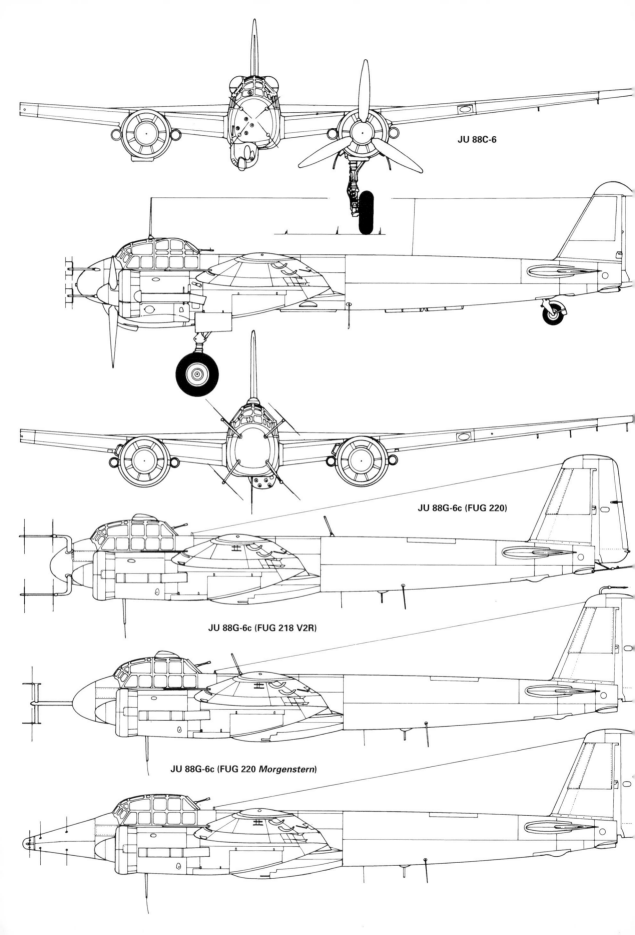

JU 88C-6

JU 88G-6c (FUG 220)

JU 88G-6c (FUG 218 V2R)

JU 88G-6c (FUG 220 *Morgenstern*)

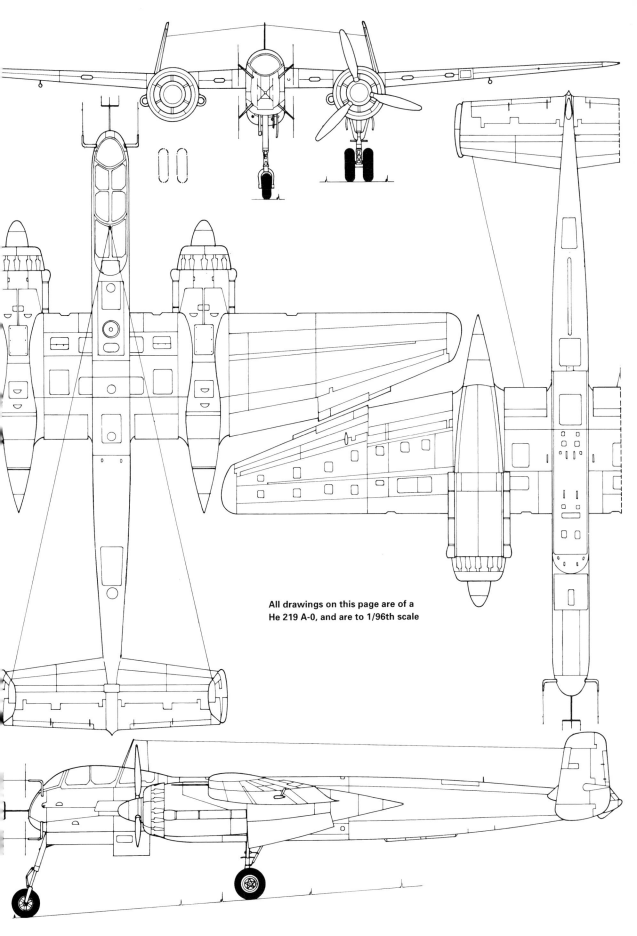

All drawings on this page are of a
He 219 A-0, and are to 1/96th scale

COLOUR PLATES

1

Bf 110C (Wk-Nr 3920) 'G9+GA' of Major Wolfgang Falck, *Geschwaderkommodore* NJG 1, Arnhem, Autumn 1940

As the original *Geschwaderkommodore* of NJG 1, Falck flew this aircraft, believed to be his first machine in nightfighter finish, from Arnhem-Deelen during the autumn of 1940. Previously credited with seven victories as a *Zerstörer* pilot with ZG 1, Falck's staff duties with NJG 1 allowed him no further chance to improve on his score, although he did fly a number of Bf 110s during the course of a long and distinguished career. The extra kill is something of a mystery, and may have been scored by another pilot.

2

Bf 110C 'G9+AA' of Oberst Wolfgang Falck, *Geschwaderkommodore* NJG 1, Holland, June 1943

Promoted to the rank of Oberst, Falck was *Geschwaderkommodore* of NJG 1 until 30 June 1943. This aircraft shows typical nightfighter markings of the period, there being less colour in regard to *Staffel* letters and so forth than in other branches of the Luftwaffe, as high visibility was hardly necessary.

3

Bf 110G-4 'G9+AA' of Oberst Hans-Joachim Jabs, *Geschwaderkommodore* NJG 1, Lüneburg, May 1945

As *Geschwaderkommodore* of NJG 1 from March 1944 to May 1945, Jabs followed the standard practice of flying an aircraft with appropriate identification letters signifying his rank and position – the double chevron denoting his rank also persisted. This aircraft, fitted with FuG 218 *Neptun* radar, had unusually, no flame damper shrouds. The *Schräge Musik* installation in the rear cockpit location was common on the Bf 110. Jabs flew only with NJG 1.

4

Bf 110G-4 'G9+AB' of Hauptmann Werner Streib, *Gruppenkommandeur* I./NJG 1, Venlo, March 1941

As *Geschwaderkommodore* of NJG 1 at Venlo, Holland, from July 1943, Streib continued to fly a black Bf 110 in similar markings to the aircraft he had originally flown in 1940. He was later instrumental in changing night fighter colouring to a completely opposite light overall shade.

5

He 219 V9 'G9+FB' of Major Werner Streib, *Gruppenkommandeur* Stab./NJG 1, Venlo, June 1943

As *Gruppenkommandeur* of NJG 1 at Venlo in July 1943, Streib was directed to form a small sub-unit in NJG 1 to prove the He 219 in combat. This aircraft, used by Streib for the type's initial combat sortie, was destroyed in a crash landing at the end of sortie in which the *Experte* had shot down five bombers. Not visible in this profile is the double chevron denoting Streib's rank, painted aft of the cockpit.

6

Bf 110C 'G9+HL' of Oberst Werner Streib, *Staffelkapitän* 2./NJG 1, Gütersloh, July 1940

As *Staffelkapitän* of 2./NJG 1 at Gutersloh in July 1940, Streib flew this partially-marked machine still with its 3.*Staffel* detailing and day fighter finish. This practise was not unusual in the days when the night fighter force was equipped almost entirely with ex-*Zerstörer* Bf 110s.

7

Bf 110C 'G9+AC' of Hauptmann Walter Ehle, *Gruppenkommandeur* II./NJG 1, Arnhem-Deelen, October 1940

As the *Gruppenkommandeur* of II./NJG 1 at Arnhem-Deelen in October 1940, Ehle was another pilot who had his rank chevron painted on his allocated aircraft. He flew all his night operations with NJG 1, and adding 35 night kills to the 3 he had previously achieved as a *Zerstörer* pilot, the first two of which were over Poland in 1939. These, plus his first six night kills, are painted on the fin of this machine, as is the common Roman 'II' aft of the badge, indicating the second *Gruppe*.

8

Bf 110E-2 'G9+BC' of Leutnant Gustav Ullenbeck, *Gruppen-Adjutant* II./NJG 1, Arnhem-Deelen, Spring 1941

Ullenbeck flew with ZG 76 in the Battle of Britain, during which he fired inconclusively at a Spitfire, before transferring to NJG 1. The aircraft depicted here was downed by flak on 9 May 1941 over Schleswig-Holstein, both occupants apparently escaping injury in the controlled belly-landing. Doubtless, signals were exchanged between the flak unit and NJG 1 – although the attentions of 'friendly fire' remained a constant hazard to the German night fighters. Despite Ullenbeck's aircraft being widely photographed, he is not known to have scored any night kills.

9

Bf 110C 'G9+BM' of Oberfeldwebel Hans Rasper, 4./NJG 1, Bergen, November 1940

While serving with NJG 1, based at Bergen, in November 1940, Rasper had his first two victories marked on the fin of his allocated aircraft, as was more or less standard practise with *Nachtjagd* Bf 110s. The 'Englandblitz' badge under the windscreen on both sides was also a common marking. Later flying with NJG 101, Rasper was credited with 8 night kills.

10

Bf 110C 'G9+LN' of Oberleutnant Heinz-Wolfgang Schnaufer, 5./NJG 1, St Trond, Summer 1942

As a member of 5./NJG 1, based at St Trond, in Belgium, in the summer of 1942, future *Experte* Schnaufer had yet to score his first kill – but this came within a matter of weeks. The aircraft bears the relatively short-lived yellow rear fuselage band, which obviously compromised night camouflage, but was probably applied to assist visibility during the twilight and early morning sorties that the *Nachtjagd* tended to fly during its first weeks in existence. Schnaufer remained with NJG 1 until October 1944, when he transferred to NJG 4.

11

Bf 110C 'G9+GP' of Leutnant Helmut Niklas, 6./NJG 1, St Trond, May 1942

Operating from St Trond in May 1942, Niklas flew a standard Bf 110C, this particular machine bearing the single victory bar denoting his first kill – a significant milestone for any combat pilot. Flying with NJG 1, and later NJG 3, Niklas scored 8 victories. He was killed on 30 January 1944 during a period of heavy casualties for the *Nachtjagd*.

12

Bf 110G-4 'G9+WD' of Oberleutnant Martin Drewes, *Gruppenkommandeur* III./NJG 1, Laon-Athies, March 1944

Kommandeur of III.*Gruppe* NJG 1, based at Laon-Athies, in France, Drewes had his-then current 22 victories painted on the fin of this aircraft – a small individual touch was the rendering of a Knight's Cross above the scoreboard. The aircraft carried FuG 220 SN-2b and FuG 218 *Lichtenstein* C1 radars. Joining the *Nachtjagd* with two *Zerst*örer kills, Drewes transferred to NJG 1 and stayed with the unit for the remainder of his service, scoring a grand total of 47 night victories.

13

Bf 110G 'G9+EF' of Major Heinz-Wolfgang Schnaufer, *Gruppenkommandeur* IV./NJG 1, St Trond, October 1944

Gruppenkommandeur of IV./NJG 1 between March and October 1944, Schnaufer took his tally to 100 kills during this period. These were duly applied to the fin of his aircraft,. which was fully equipped with FuG 220 SN-2 radar and *Schräge Musik*.

14

Bf 110G-4 'G9+EZ' of Oberleutnant Heinz-Wolfgang Schnaufer, *Staffelkapitän* 12./NJG 1, St Trond, February 1944

As *Staffelkapitän* of 12./NJG 1 in February 1944, Schnaufer used this Bf 110G-4, fitted with FuG 202 radar, an extended barrel nose cannon and *Schräge Musik*. The aircraft bears a tally of 47 kills scored by Schnaufer up to that time, his most recent being on the night of the 14th. Captured by the British at Grove, in Denmark, in May 1945, Schnaufer was interrogated and eventually allowed to return home.

15

Ju 88C-6 'R4+XM' of Major Prinz Heinrich zu Sayn-Wittgenstein, *Geschwaderkommodore* NJG 2, Stendal, January 1944

Kommodore of NJG 2 from 1 January 1944 until his death on the 21st, Sayn-Wittgenstein had his own aircraft allocated, but this machine had previously been damaged in combat and the prince borrowed another Ju 88 for the sortie on the night he died – this standard 4.*Staffel* C-6 may well have been that aircraft. With the unit at Stendal, Germany, in January 1944, it boasted FuG 202 and FuG 220 SN-2 radar

16

Ju 88C-2 'R4+KL' of Leutnant Alfons Köster, 1./NJG 2, Gilze-Rijen, October 1941

1./NJG 2 was based at Gilze-Rijen, Holland, in October 1941 and engaged primarily on intruder duties, for which a black paint scheme with national insignia overpainted to complete the camouflage effect was ideal. Relatively few Luftwaffe units went to such lengths to hide their presence over enemy territory, but the cloak of anonomity yielded good results for the unit. Koster's successful career as an intruder pilot brought him 25 kills, his service career also taking in periods with NJGs 1 and 3 before he was killed on 7 January 1945.

17

Do 17Z-10 'R4+AK' of Hauptmann Erich Jung,

Staffelkapitän 2./NJG 2, Gilze-Rijen, Autumn 1940

Again sporting the all-black paint finish adopted for the *Nachtjagd* virtually from its formation, the early Dornier night fighters were issued to a number of units, where they tended to back up the Ju 88s and Bf 110s – this example carried the *Spanner* infra-red sight. The grey code letters are relieved by virtually the only spots of colour on the aircraft – the red spinner tips, signifying the *Staffel*. Jung was the *Staffelkapitän* while the unit operated from Gilze-Rijen during the autumn of 1940. Flying only with NJG 2, he scored 28 victories at night.

18

Ju 88C-2 'R4+CK' of Leutnant Heinz Rökker, 2./NJG 2, Catania, 1942

When NJG 2 moved from Europe to Catania, Sicily, its aircraft adopted the theatre marking of a white rear fuselage band, which stood out boldly against the black overall paint. Rökker appears not to have marked his victories on this aircraft during the period, although he ultimately shot down 64 aircraft exclusively with NJG 2.

19

Do 215B-5 'R4+DC' of Oberleutnant Helmut Lent, *Gruppenkommandeur* II./NJG 2, Leeuwarden, 1942

A FuG 202-equipped aircraft in one of the non-standard 'factory' finishes applied to its night fighter variants by Dornier, this Do 215 also has an additional belly pack for the MG FF cannon. Photographic evidence would indicate that these exotic schemes, along with broadly interpreted *Balkenkreuz* dimensions, were not always painted over in 'regulation' colours for night fighters. The *Gruppenkommandeur* of II./NJG 2 at Leewauden from November 1941 to October 1942, Lent was second only to Schnaufer in terms of night victories.

20

Ju 88C-6 'R4+AC' of Hauptmann Dr Horst Patuschka, *Gruppenkommandeur* II./NJG 2, Comiso, Early 1943

By deleting the letter indicating the *Staffel* and merely chalking in the inividual aircraft letter for flight line indentification, the unit's groundcrew did all they could to 'hide' their Ju 88 charges from unauthorised eyes. But as the *Kommandeur* of II./NJG 2, Patuschka was entitled to put up his current victory total during operations from Comiso, Sicily, early in 1943. Serving only with NJG 2, Patuschka scored 23 victories before being killed in action (possibly in this very aircraft, Wk-Nr 360226) over Bizerte, Tunisia, on 6 March 1943.

21

Ju 88G-1 'R4+AC' of Major Paul Semrau, *Gruppenkommandeur* II./NJG 2, Kassel-Rothwesten, Spring 1944

Semrau was *Gruppenkommandeur* of II.*Gruppe* between January and November 1944, when it operated from Kassel-Rothwesten, Germany. Although it bears no victory markings on the port side, Semrau's aircraft shows some individuality in that its nose armament had extended cannon barrels, one of numerous weapons variations possible with the G-series, which included the twin 20 mm belly pack shown here. The radar is SN-2, with FuG 227 *Flensburg* aerials on the wings. Another pilot who spent all his career with NJG 2, Semrau had scored 46 kills prior to death in action on 8 February 1945.

22

Ju 88G-6 '4R+AN' of Oberleutnant Erich Jung, 5./NJG 2, Mainz-Finthen, March 1945

Flying a Ju 88 throughout his service with NJG 2, Erich Jung too served only with this one unit. Operating with 5./NJG 2 from Mainz-Finthen, Germany, in March 1945, Jung's aircraft had SN-2, FuG 220 tail warning radar and twin *Schräge Musik* cannon in the mid fuselage point, one of three optional installations on the Ju 88G series. It also had the 'reversed' code '4R' rather than 'R4', which was quite common in NJG 5 from 1944 onwards. Jung scored 28 victories

23

Ju 88G-6 (Wk-Nr 622330) '4R+BR' of Oberleutnant Walter Briegleb, *Staffelkapitän* 7./NJG 2, Kassel-Rothwesten, Autumn 1944

Fitted with SN-2, FuG 220 and a forward *Schräge Musik* installation, this Ju 88 has its victory bars applied on the fin – a location favoured by most of the *Experten* known to have flown this type. By contrast to some of the early Ju 88s, Briegleb's G-6 was quite extensively marked, as was the perogative of a *Staffelkapitän*. Leading 7./NJG 2 while it was based at Kassel-Rothwesten during the autumn of 1944, Briegleb later transferred to NJG 3 but the score of 25 kills displayed here was not improved upon.

24

Bf 110C 'D5+AS' of Oberleutnant Walter Borchers, *Staffelkapitän* 8./NJG 3, Lüneburg, Winter 1941-42

Borchers was the Staffelkapitän of 8./NJG 3 while it was stationed at Lüneberg, Germany, during the winter of 1941-42. At that time, his aircraft carried night fighter codes over the retained *Zerstörer* finish, complete with the 'Haifisch' marking widely used by II./ZG 76. This Bf 110 also kept the yellow band associated with the early night fighter force. To 11 kills as a *Zerstörer* pilot, Borchers added another 48 at night while serving with NJGs 3 and 5. He was killed on 5 March 1945.

25

Bf 110G-4 'G9+BA' of Major Heinz-Wolfgang Schnaufer, *Geschwaderkommodore* NJG 4, Schleswig, March 1945

An anomaly in that it apparently had the Stab marking 'A' rather than the individual aircraft letter in green, this aircraft was the last Bf 110 flown by the leading *Nachtjagd Experte*. When the war finished he was *Geschwaderkommodore* of NJG 4 , operating from Grove, in Denmark. This aircraft was fitted with FuG 218 *Neptun* radar and had the late war *Eberspacher* single pipe flame damping exhausts. Schnaufer and his unit's Bf 110s were captured by the British, who reportedly had this aircraft brought to England and put on public display in Hyde Park – quite understandably, given these provocative markings. Today, only the port fin survives.

26

Bf 110G '3C+MK' of Oberleutnant Martin Becker, 2./NJG 4, Florennes, Summer 1944

Based at Florrenes, France, during the summer of 1944, this SN-2b-equipped aircraft had an unusual treatment of the *Balkenkreuz* in that it had apparently been oversprayed and then partially re-applied in the form of a thin, dark grey outline. Becker's score at that time was 30, and these are represent-

ed on the fin in the usual style, but without the diagonal 'stripe', which in some instances was actually the pilot's name. Serving with NJGs 3, 4 and 6, Becker scored 53 kills.

27

Bf 110F '3C+AR' of Oberleutnant Hans-Karl Kamp, *Staffelkapitän* 7./NJG 4, Mainz-Finthen, Summer 1942

Another black Bf 110 in standard markings with grey codes. The individual aircraft letter was usually repeated on the extreme nose for the benefit of the groundcrew, and this machine has a dual *Staffel*/additional safety aid in that the tips of the spinners are painted white – it helped to see at least part of the aircraft if it was lined up on a dark dispersal with about a dozen others! Kamp was *Staffelkapitän* of 7./NJG 4, which flew from from Mainz-Finthen during the summer of 1942. He later transferred to JG 300 and had scored 23 kills by the time of his death on 31 December 1944.

28

Bf 110C '3C+LR' of Oberfeldwebel Reinhard Kollack, 7./NJG 4, Mainz-Finthen, Summer 1942

The common use of a white outline for the individual aircraft letter on black finish is shown here, this letter often being repeated on both the extreme nose and the leading edges of both wings inboard of the engines. Flying with 7./NJG 4 from Mainz-Finthen during mid-1942, Kollack had ten kills at that time. Early night fighter scores were represented by white bars without the detail applied later. Kollack ended the war with 49 kills, accumulated during service with NJGs 1 and 4.

29

Ju 88G-6 'C9+AA' of Maj Rudolf Schoenert, *Geschwaderkommandeur* NJG 5, location unknown, Spring 1945

Geschwaderkommodore of NJG 5 from March to May 1945, Schoenert almost certainly had another aircraft that he flew regularly, this example being something of a radar test bed in NJG 5. Neither the rear fuselage aerial configuration for SN-2 or the tail warning radar was standard, although the aircraft also had SN-2 nose radar aerials. A 64-victory *Experte*, Schoenert flew with NJGs 1, 2, 5 and 100.

30

Bf 110G-4 'C9+AC' of Oberleutnant Leopold Fellerer, *Gruppenkommandeur* II./NJG 5, Gütersloh, January 1944

Gruppenkommandeur of II./NJG 5 from January to May 1944, Fellerer's unit operated from Gütersloh, Germany, in January when this aircraft was on strength. It exhibits some variation in the 22 victory bars in that two of them lack the diagonal stripe detail, possibly to indicate daylight kills. A FuG 202 *Lichtenstein BC* radar is fitted. Flying with NJGs 1, 5 and 6, Fellerer scored a total of 41 kills, his last Bf 110G, complete with decorated tailfin, being discovered by US troops.

31

Ju 88G-6 'C9+AC' of Major Hans Leickhardt, *Gruppenkommandeur* II./NJG 5, Hagenau, late 1944

Gruppenkommandeur of II./NJG 5 from May 1944 to March 1945, Leickhardt's machine is shown when operating from Magenau circa winter 1944-45. Leickhardt was apparently one of relatively few pilots to fly a Ju 88 in combat equipped with the latest *Morgenstern* radar. His aircraft bears a camouflage scheme that departed from previous 'standard' night fighter colours, but a general change was in evidence in the last months of the war. Victor over 30 aircraft, Leickhardt flew with NJGs 1 and 5. He was killed on 5 March 1945.

32

Bf 110G-4 'C9+EN' of Oberleutnant Wilhelm Johnen, *Staffelkapitän* of 5./NJG 5, Hagenau, April 1944

Author of *Duel Under the Stars*, one of the few first-hand records of the *Nachtjagd* published in English, Johnen achieved some notoriety by landing this aircraft, fully equipped with SN-2b and FuG 218 C1 radar, in Switzerland in 1944. Its densely mottled fuselage was a variation in the generally-applied lighter schemes in vogue with the *Nachtjagd* at that time, but darker schemes in disruptive patterns were becoming popular. Johnen scored 34 victories and served with NJGs 1, 5 and 6.

33

Bf 110G-4 'C9+AD' of Major Paul Zorner, *Gruppenkommandeur* III./NJG 5, location unknown, mid 1944

Gruppenkommandeur of III./NJG 5 from March to October1944, Paul Zorner was a highly skilled pilot dedicated to the *Nachtjagd*. His aircraft, fitted with FuG 220 SN-2b and *Schräge Musik*, could be said to reflect considerable pride in his branch of the Luftwaffe, the markings hardly being intended for either anonimity or concealment! Shown at a time when he had marked 42 kills on his aircraft, Zorner's final tally reached 59. His wartime service encompassed NJGs 2, 3, 5 and 100.

34

Bf 110G-4 'C9+AD' of Hauptmann Ulrich von Meien, *Gruppenkommandeur* III./NJG 5, Königsberg, winter 1944-45

As replacement for Paul Zorner as *Gruppenkommandeur* of III./NJG 5, von Meien flew a similarly-marked Bf 110 to that of his illustrious predecessor from Königsberg during the winter of 1944-45. An aircraft that represents almost the final paint finish for the Bf 110G, the fighter has a long-barrelled MG 151 nose cannon with flash suppressor, plus FuG 220 SN-2b and FuG 218 C1 radar. One of the pilots who flew with some of the lesser-known night fighter formations, von Meien scored nine victories during a career that took in service with NJGs 100 and 200, and finally, NJG 5.

35

Ju 88C-6 'C9+DE' of Hauptmann Prinz Heinrich zu Sayn-Wittgenstein, *Gruppenkommandeur* IV./NJG 5, Leipheim, early 1943

With its standard paintwork considerably dulled down, Sayn-Wittgenstein's victory tally had a number of linked victory bars, almost certainly indicating multiple kills in a single night. Applying these across the *Hakenkreuz* was a common enough practise in Ju 88 nightfighter units. Again the yellow fuselage band was applied to give some form of recognition on the ground and standard FuG 202 *Lichtenstein* C1 radar was fitted. The *Gruppenkommandeur* of IV./NJG 5 from late 1942 until August 1943 when it became I./NJG 100, the 'fighting prince' was a totally dedicated exponent of the *Nachtjagd* in general, and the Ju 88 in particular.

36

Ju 88G-6 'C9+AE' of Hauptmann Rudolf Altendorff, *Gruppenkommandeur* IV./NJG 5, Langensabza, Autumn 1944

A Ju 88 in the most common overall camouflage for this type in the mid-1944 period, Altendorff's aircraft had aft-mounted *Schräge Musik*, SN-2 and FuG 220 tail warning radar. In common with a number of other pilots, Altendorff applied a rank chevron forward of the fuselage unit codes. He was *Gruppenkommandeur* of IV./NJG 5 when it operated from Langensbza in March 1944. With 25 night victories to his credit, Altendorff flew with NJGs 3, 4 and 5.

37

Bf 110G-2 '2Z+AC' of Hauptmann Rolf Leuchs, *Gruppenkommandeur* II./NJG 6, Echterdingen, March 1944

One of many Bf 110s that flew in camouflage more associated with *Zerstörers* than nightfighters, Leuchs' machine was unusual in that three shades of grey-green paint rather than the normal two were applied to the top surfaces. The aircraft was also unusual in having the early style Bf 110F vertical tail surfaces rather than the broad chord rudders of the G series, although this configuration was intended to be standard on variants fitted with FuG 202 radar. As *Gruppenkommandeur* of II./NJG 6 operating from Echterdingen during March 1944, Leuchs served only with NJG 6, and scored 10 victories.

38

Ju 88G-6 'W7+AC' of Major Paul Zorner, *Gruppenkommandeur* II./NJG 100, Stubendorf, late 1944

Another rather plain Ju 88G fitted with FuG 220 and forward *Schräge Musik*, this example does not reflect the substantial victory tally already accrued by its pilot. Taking over as *Gruppenkommandeur* of II./NJG 100 in July 1944, Zorner's unit was operating from Stubendorf, Germany, by late 1944. The original Eastern Front night fighter Geschwader, NJG 100's movements reflected Germany's waxing fortunes in the ill-fated campaign against the Russians.

39

Bf 109G-6 'Red 6' of Oberfeldwebel Arnold Döring, 2./JG 300, location unknown, August 1943

The original '*Wilde Sau*' unit, JG 300's Bf 109s helped fill the gap caused by the Allied use of 'Window', which temporarily blinded radar and hampered the conventional night fighters. Döring's 2.*Staffel* existed from August 1943, and the application of black paint over standard day fighter markings was relatively unusual. Unusual himself in that he scored his first ten victories as a bomber pilot with KGs 53 and 55, Döring transferred to the '*Wilde Sau*' force and also flew with II./JG 300, before another change to NJG 2 and finally NJG 3. For earlier examples of a Bf 109 and Fw 190 night fighter see *Aircraft of the Aces 11 - Bf 109D/E Aces 1939-40* (profile 11) and *Aircraft of the Aces 9 - Fw 190 Aces of the Western Front* (profile 9) respectively.

40

Bf 109G-14 'Green 3' of Major Friedrich-Karl Müller, *Gruppenkommandeur* of I./NJG 11, Werneuchen, late 1944

In standard day fighter camouflage and markings, Müller's aircraft emphasises the dual role undertaken by the '*Wilde Sau*' units at war's end. With the conventional *Nachtjagd* coping with night raids, the use of day fighters at night waned – there was more than enough for them to do during daylight hours! As *Gruppenkommandeur* of I./NJG 11 flying from Werneuchen, Germany, in late 1944, Müller's 30 victories marked him as one of the leading '*Wilde Sau*' pilot of the war. He had served with JG 300 and NJGr 10 before transferring to NJG 11. Müller's 'Green 3' scheme was resurrected in 1995 when German warbird enthusiast Hans Dittes had his recently restored Bf 109G-10 'hybrid' (the aircraft is an amalgamation of fuselage, undercarriage, propeller and cowling parts from G-10 Wk-Nr 151591, married to the wings of a G-6 instructional airframe supplied to Spain during World War 2, and powered by a DB 605D-1 engine found in a bricked-up room in a swimwear factory near Turin!) painted in the colours of the night fighter ace. It was subsequently operated in England by The Old Flying Machine Company, before being returned to Germany in late 1996. For an example of an Me 262 nightfighter of NJG 11's 10.*Staffel* see *Aircraft of the Aces 17 - German Jet Aces of World War 2*.

FIGURE PLATES

1

Hauptmann Heinrich Prinz zu Sayn-Wittgenstein, *Gruppenkommandeur* of II./NJG 3 at Schleswig in August 1943. Pictured in regulation lightweight summer tunic and standard issue officer's cap, breeches and boots, Hauptmann Prinz zu Sayn-Wittgenstein's only concession to individuality is the civilian scarf framing the Knight's Cross around his neck. He had received this award on 2 October 1942 for 22 night kills. On the last day of August 1943, after claiming another 25 victories, he would be presented with the Oak Leaves. He celebrated his promotion to Kommodore of NJG 2 on 1 January 1944 by scoring six kills that same night. Three weeks later, on 21 January, he almost repeated this feat, but was himself shot down by an RAF night fighter after claiming his fifth bomber in succession. His final total of 83 victories made him the Luftwaffe's third most successful night-fighter pilot and earned him the Swords posthumously.

2

Major Wolfgang Falck, *Geschwaderkommodore* of NJG 1 at Arnhem in October 1940. Wolfgang Falck is seen here wearing multi-zippered summer pattern flying overalls with officer's service cap, standard issue flying boots and an Fl 301542 inflatable life-jacket with both mouth-piece (top) and compressed air cylinder at waist. Note the Major's cloth rank patches on both sleeves (compare with the Hauptmann's, left). Falck, too, displays the Knight's Cross, awarded primarily for his qualities of leadership. For although he was credited with seven previous kills as a *Zerstörer* pilot, he did not make nocturnal ace. He was, however, responsible for laying the foundations of the night fighter arm; setting up NJG 1 in June 1940 and serving as its Kommodore for over three years. He spent the remainder of the war in a variety of staff positions.

3

Hauptmann Werner Streib, *Gruppenkommandeur* of I./NJG 1 at Gilze-Rijen in the winter of 1941-42. Snug in two-piece winter heated overalls (note connecting elements above left cuff), flying helmet, boots and Fl 30156 kapok life-jacket,

Streib was Falck's communications officer in I./ZG 1 before following him into NJG 1. After long service at the head of I.*Gruppe*, he succeeded Falck as *Geschwaderkommodore* of NJG 1 on 1 July 1943. From 1 March 1944 until the end of the war, Oberstleutnant Werner Streib held the office of Inspector of Night Fighters. Credited with the Luftwaffe's first official night victory (on 20 July 1940), Streib subsequently added another 64 during a frontline career which also earned him the Oak Leaves and Swords to the Knight's Cross pictured here.

4

Hauptmann Leopold Fellerer, *Gruppenkommandeur* of II./NJG 5 at Leipheim in March 1944. Relaxing with a post-operational cigar, Austrian-born "Poldi" Fellerer looks even more comfortable with his service dress tunic tucked into "baggy" flight trousers, with deep patch pockets and worn with flying boots and the officer's pattern gabardine *Feldmütze* field service forage cap, more colloquially know as a *Schiffchen* (little ship). Note, too, the pilot's badge and Iron Cross, First Class, on his left breast and the white, green, red signalling torch on the lanyard around his neck. The latter was soon to be replaced by a Knight's Cross, awarded on 8 April 1944 for 28 night kills. By the war's end Fellerer's score would have risen to 41 (including two claimed during hazardous daylight missions).

5

Major Helmut Lent, *Geschwaderkommodore* of NJG 3 at Stade in August 1943. Cutting a more formal figure, as befits the night-fighter arm's second-highest scorer, Major Helmut Lent opts for a black leather Luftwaffe flying jacket with standard dress trousers and shoes. Note the lightweight mesh flying helmet (*Netzkopfhaube*) with throat microphone and tinted goggles. Another graduate from the daylight *Zerstörer*, Lent here displays the Swords and Oak Leaves to his Knight's Cross. On 31 July 1944 he would receive the Diamonds as the first night fighter pilot to reach the century. With a final score standing at 102 night kills (plus 11 earlier *Zerstörer* victories), Lent died on 7 October 1944 from injuries sustained two days earlier when his aircraft suffered engine failure as he was coming in to land at Paderborn and crashed after hitting high-tension cables.

6

Oberleutnant Heinz-Wolfgang Schnaufer, *Staffelkapitän* of 12./NJG 1 at Leeuwarden in January 1944. The most successful of them all, Schnaufer is depicted here in standard officer's tunic, breeches and flying boots, and wearing his favoured headgear, a 1943 pattern soft cap. Note the Iron Cross, First Class, on his left breast pocket, the German Cross on the right, and the newly awarded Knight's Cross at his neck. A relative latecomer, Schnaufer's first kill was claimed on 2 June 1942. By the end of hostilities, which saw him as *Geschwaderkommodore* of NJG 4, he had amassed a staggering 121 night kills in 164 operational missions. By a strange coincidence, although he survived the war, Schnaufer was to suffer the same fate as Lent; succumbing to injuries two days after being involved in a crash – in his case a road accident while driving along a straight road through a forest on a business trip in France on 13 July 1950. His car was in collision with a truck, which had turned out of a side road.